The Book On Clarity

How to Think Cleanly in a Messy World

The Book On Series

Avery Keene

Published by The Book On Publishing, 2025.
First edition. July 30, 2025.

Website: https://thebookon.ca
Substack: https://thebookonpublishing.substack.com/

The Book On Clarity: How to Think Cleanly in a Messy World

First edition. July 30, 2025.

Copyright © 2025 The Book On Publishing
ISBN: 978-1-997795-71-1

Written by Avery Keene

The Book On Series

Read This First

This is not a book designed to entertain you. It's not here to charm, to soothe, or to hold your hand. It won't dazzle you with stories, metaphors, or motivational fluff. What you're having is a tool, an instruction manual written for people who are serious about learning, executing, and thinking at a higher level.

Every book in The Book On Series is built on a single premise: clarity beats complexity. We believe that when you strip away the noise, the emotions, the marketing spin, and the cultural rituals of "self-help," what's left is raw, unembellished instruction. That's what these books offer.

They are dry by design. Not because we don't care about language or narrative, but because when you're building something that matters, you don't need more distractions. You need a clear architecture. Mental scaffolding. Direction that respects your intelligence.

Each title in this series takes on a specific domain: decision-making, clarity, strategy, leverage, and uncertainty, and drills deep, not in sweeping generalizations, but in applied frameworks. These are books for builders, operators, founders, tacticians, and thinkers—people who don't just consume knowledge but operationalize it.

You'll find no chapter-long anecdotes here. No self-congratulatory memoirs. No bullet-point platitudes. Instead, what you'll get is structured insight: argument, example, application. The tone is direct. The prose is sober. The ideas are designed to be lifted out and used.

You won't be coddled, but you won't be misled either.

There's a place in the world for lyrical, emotional, story-driven books, and this isn't that place. This is a workspace. A blueprint. A conversation for people who are ready to act, not just absorb.

We respect your time and your intellect.

Welcome to The Book On Series.

Table of Contents

Dedication

To those who've been gaslit by noise,

Who've been told their confusion is a flaw instead

of a consequence,

And who still tries, against all odds, to think

cleanly in a world designed to distort.

This is for you.

You were never broken. The signal was just buried.

- Avery

Acknowledgement

This book wouldn't exist without the conversations I've had with people brave enough to admit they couldn't see straight. Friends, readers, strangers, some of you sent one sentence by email, others sat with me over coffee and chaos. You gave voice to something I was still untangling in myself: that modern life doesn't just move fast, it blurs. And underneath our hustle for certainty lies a deeper hunger for clarity.

To the thinkers who refuse to self-censor, who keep refining their inner lens instead of projecting their pain outward, thank you. Your work doesn't trend. It doesn't go viral. But it keeps the world sane.

To those who helped shape this manuscript by challenging me, editing with precision, or simply asking better questions than I had answers, your fingerprints are on every page. This is a book built in conversation, and it belongs as much to the unseen as it does to the author.

And to the version of me that had to write through fog to find form: I'm glad you stayed the course.

Preface

When Thinking Stops Working

There are moments when your brain turns against you, not in the dramatic, collapsing-into-panic way, but in the quiet, insidious erosion of certainty. You sit at your desk, or in your car, or across the table from someone you love, and you realize you don't know what you think anymore. Not clearly. Not cleanly. You hear echoes, feel emotions, replay scripts. But clarity? That feels distant. Muffled. Like you're trying to tune a radio station that used to come in strong, and now only gives you static.

I've lived long enough and thought hard enough to know this isn't personal failure. It's systemic. The modern world is not built for clarity. It is built for consumption. For reaction. For speed. And clarity, by its nature, resists all three. Clarity slows you down. It costs energy. It demands silence. It asks you to admit what you've been avoiding. And sometimes, it makes you let go of the narratives that got you through the last five years, because now, they're standing in the way.

This is not a book about thinking better. It's a book about thinking **cleaner**.

That distinction matters. Better implies more, more logic, more frameworks, more cleverness. Clean is different. Clean cuts away. Clean thinking isn't louder or more impressive. It's more honest. More discerning. More aligned with reality, even when the truth is uncomfortable.

You don't need more input. You need to learn which signals to trust. Which distortions to ignore? And how to create enough inner space to hear yourself think again. That's what this book is for.

We'll start in the fog, because that's where most of us live. Then we'll learn how to build clarity not as a momentary breakthrough, but as a way of navigating. And finally, we'll examine how to sustain it, how to lead with it, and how to protect it in a world that's incentivized to steal it back.

There are no formulas here—just a framework for reclaiming your lens.

Think of clarity not as a single breakthrough, but as a sequence: *Fog → Filtration → Framework → Feedback → Embodiment*. First, we name the fog, the distortion, the distraction, and the emotional static clouding our thinking. Then, we filter, clearing the noise from the signal. With space regained, we build frameworks that hold insight, refine our internal feedback systems, and finally, root our clarity in action, presence, and body. This isn't a formula. It's a cycle. One you'll return to, over and over, as the world keeps pulling you away from yourself.

The world may not get cleaner. But your mind can.

Let's begin.

Part I, The Fog

Chapter 1: The Clarity Deficit

You don't notice you've lost clarity until the moment you need it most. One minute you're moving through life on what feels like solid ground, and the next, you're caught in the undertow of your thoughts. You hesitate. You doubt. You play out four competing options in your head, none of them clean, none of them confident. And then, without quite realizing it, you default. You pick the familiar, the reactive, or the convenient, not because it's right, but because your brain wants the discomfort to stop.

That is the cost of the clarity deficit.

We live in an era of hyper-stimulation, perpetual distraction, and ideological whiplash. But beneath all that noise is a more dangerous and less talked-about phenomenon: our declining ability to think with precision. Not intelligence, there's no shortage of that. We have more information than any generation in human history. What we're losing is **clarity**: the ability to perceive reality cleanly, to discern what matters, and to make decisions with integrity.

Clarity isn't the same as certainty. Certainty is often a false god, an illusion wrapped in bravado. Clarity is different. It's not about being sure. It's about being honest. Honest about what you know, what you feel, and what you're seeing, not what you want to see. Clarity doesn't guarantee you'll make the perfect decision. It guarantees you'll make the real one. The one that's yours.

But that kind of thinking is rare now. What passes for clarity is often just alignment with someone else's framework. We outsource our priorities to algorithms. We parrot someone else's conclusions because they had the confidence to say it first. We confuse speed for decisiveness, eloquence for insight, and branding for truth. And over time, we become mentally threadbare, making more decisions, but with less conviction. Churning through inputs without ever metabolizing them.

What does this look like in real life? It seems that staying in relationships that feel wrong is preferable to leaving, as leaving can be murkier. It looks like hesitating on a business move, not because it's bad, but because the fog in your head makes everything feel equally risky. It seems like obsessively researching the "best" diet, strategy, job, or tool, not because you care about quality, but because you're terrified of regret. That's not discernment. That's paralysis masquerading as prudence.

The clarity deficit shows up everywhere. In our inability to make decisions, we can stand behind. In our emotional reactivity when presented with new ideas. In our growing intolerance for ambiguity, nuance, or complexity. And worst of all, in our increasing comfort with mental shortcuts that don't serve us, but do make the moment pass.

Why is this happening? Part of it is technological. We are in a constant stream of input, news, feeds, updates, and alerts. Our brains were not designed to process this much signal without scrambling. But it's also cultural. We reward speed over reflection. We treat ambiguity like failure. We shame indecision even when the stakes are unclear. We expect ourselves to have strong takes, hot takes, branded takes, even when we haven't sat with a question long enough to form an honest opinion.

In this environment, clarity isn't just difficult. It's subversive.

To think cleanly now is to swim against a very profitable current. The market doesn't benefit when you pause to think. The system doesn't reward your internal alignment. What it wants is engagement, now, loud, and continuous. So it bombards you with a thousand urgent half-truths and trains your mind to mistake noise for signal. Eventually, the static becomes your default.

You wake up not knowing what you care about. You finish a conversation, unsure of what you even said. You pursue goals that once lit you up but now feel suspiciously like someone else's dreams. This is the real consequence of the clarity deficit: you become the executor of ideas you didn't choose.

And clarity is always a choice. Not a given, not a gift, not a personality trait. A choice. A practice. Something you cultivate not once, but daily. Something you return to, over and over, when the fog starts creeping in.

So how do we start?

Not with more information. Not with better opinions. We start by noticing the fog, which makes us admit that we don't see clearly. By naming the drag we feel when we try to make decisions. We start by questioning our inputs, our defaults, and our sacred cows. We begin with the possibility that our internal compass is rusted, not because we're broken, but because we've never been taught to protect it.

Clarity begins when you stop pretending you already have it.

This book is not here to give you five steps to instant enlightenment. It's not a productivity manual or a cognitive detox. It's a guide for those who suspect something's off in how they're thinking, sensing, deciding. It's for those who want to stop borrowing mental frameworks that look good online and start building a lens that works in real life.

Because without clarity, all your plans are guesses. All your actions are reactions. And all your potential gets run through a filter you didn't choose.

You can't afford that anymore. None of us can.

It's time to clean the lens.

Chapter 2: Why We Don't See Clearly

Most of us walk around assuming we're seeing the world more or less as it is. We believe our thoughts are rooted in facts, our feelings are grounded in reality, and our interpretations, while not perfect, are at least directionally accurate. But the truth is more complicated to swallow; we rarely see things as they are. We see things as they've been filtered, distorted, framed, and colored by forces we seldom notice and rarely question.

That isn't a judgment. It's a neurological fact.

Human perception is a process of **construction**, not direct access. Your eyes don't show you the world; they show you a high-speed, heavily compressed rendering of light patterns that your brain stitches together based on experience, memory, and expectation. That rendering is good enough for walking down the street without bumping into lampposts, but it's riddled with blind spots when it comes to interpreting nuance, complexity, or meaning.

The same is true of your thoughts. You don't think in a vacuum. Every idea you form is shaped by prior beliefs, emotional state, social context, and the architecture of your attention. The brain is a pattern-matching machine, and it would rather be **fast than accurate**. That's why it jumps to conclusions. That's why it filters out data that contradicts your current worldview. That's why you can look at the same situation as someone else and walk away with a completely different conclusion, and both of you will swear yours is the "objective" one.

Let's ask the fundamental question: **Why don't we see clearly?**

There are many answers. But they tend to cluster around three primary distortions: *biological constraints*, *emotional residue*, and *environmental interference*.

First, the biology. Our brains are not wired for clarity. They're wired for survival. Clarity takes time and cognitive energy, two things that were in short supply for most of human history. Our ancestors didn't need accurate information to thrive. They needed *fast, safe guesses*. See movement? Assume predator. Hear rustling? Move away. Feel out of place? Conform. These instincts kept us alive, but they didn't evolve for truth. They became a utility. And that utility often favors simplicity over depth, certainty over nuance, and social harmony over independent thought.

Second, the emotional layer. Emotions are not the enemy of clarity, but they are often its saboteur. When we're angry, anxious, ashamed, or defensive, our capacity for clean thinking drops. Not because we lack intelligence, but because emotion warps the relevance filter. It tells us what to pay attention to, what to amplify, and what to ignore. If you're angry, you're more likely to interpret neutral events as hostile. If you're afraid, you'll overestimate risk and underestimate your ability to respond. Emotions are powerful signalers, but unless we train ourselves to interpret them correctly, they distort the lens.

Finally, the environment. And here, things get darker. Because the modern world is not just chaotic, it's actively **weaponized against clarity**. Social media platforms reward outrage, speed, and simplification. News cycles reward scandal and crisis, not subtlety or context. Online debates devolve into tribal warfare, where the goal is no longer truth, but dominance. Even our workplace tools, from email to project management systems, optimize for volume, not discernment. Every channel shouts. Every message demands your attention now.

Add to that the commodification of attention, where every brand, app, and influencer is vying to hijack your cognitive bandwidth, and you begin to realize just how hostile your environment is to clear thinking. The system is designed to pull your attention outward, fracture your focus, and drown you in inputs you didn't choose and don't need.

And because we adapt to our environment, we start to normalize the noise. We mistake being overwhelmed for being informed. We think reflexive hot takes are the same as informed opinions. We feel guilty for not having a stance on everything, even as our actual beliefs grow less coherent.

This is the slow erosion of clarity. Not a dramatic collapse, but a quiet war of attrition. A thousand micro-distortions, every day, that dull our inner lens until we no longer trust what we see, or worse, no longer notice that we've stopped seeing at all.

But clarity doesn't die in the face of distortion. It dies when we stop noticing the distortion is there.

The goal, then, is not to escape distortion; that's impossible. The goal is to **build awareness**. To see the filters, feel the fog, and catch the moment when you're no longer responding to reality, but to your preloaded interpretation of it. That's the doorway to clarity. Not certainty. Not confidence. Just awareness.

You start by asking uncomfortable questions. Where can I find what I'm looking for? What assumptions am I using to fill in the blanks? What emotions are shaping this interpretation? What incentives, personal or systemic, are bending the narrative I've accepted as accurate?

These questions don't always lead to satisfying answers. Sometimes they lead to more discomfort. But discomfort isn't the enemy either. It's a sign that your internal lens is getting recalibrated. You're shedding distortions that felt familiar. And clarity often begins with that very unease, the sense that something doesn't add up, even if you can't articulate why.

We don't see clearly because we're not taught to. We're taught to conform, to react, to signal, to survive. Clarity is a different skillset entirely. And like any skill, it has to be practiced. You don't get it once and keep it forever. You earn it every time you decide to pause, observe, and revise.

It's not always fun. It's not always fast. But it is always worth it.

Because when you start to see, even just a little, you start making decisions you can live with. You speak with more weight. You feel less like a pinball and more like a compass. You lose your addiction to drama. And you gain something rare and powerful: a mind you can trust, even when the world is screaming otherwise.

Chapter 3: The Attention War

You've probably heard that attention is your most valuable resource. But it's more than that. Attention is a *currency*. And like any currency, it gets devalued when overextended, misallocated, or traded too cheaply.

The tragedy of our time isn't just that we're distracted. It's that we've normalized distraction as our baseline. We no longer control the lens; we let it drift, flicker, and fragment until clarity becomes impossible.

To understand clarity, you have to understand attention. Not just what draws it, but what distorts it. Attention isn't passive. It's not just where you look, it's what you amplify, what you interpret, what becomes real in your internal world. When your attention is hijacked, you don't just lose focus. You lose your ability to make sense.

That's what makes this war so dangerous. It's not about productivity. It's about sovereignty over your perception.

The human brain can only consciously process a narrow stream of information. You filter constantly, choosing what gets in, what gets ignored. What you focus on becomes your working reality. The rest fades.

But here's the problem: you're not fully in charge of that filter. External actors have learned to engineer it. Social platforms, marketers, and even productivity tools profit from your diverted focus. They've refined the stimulus loop: variable rewards, artificial urgency, infinite scroll. Each design choice is calculated to short-circuit reflection and train compulsive engagement.

You think you're choosing. You're not. You're responding to cues crafted to override discernment.

And the cost isn't just time. Its depth. Every time your attention is splintered, your capacity for sustained thought, the soil of clarity, erodes. You flinch instead of focusing. You skim instead of synthesize. Eventually, you confuse motion with meaning.

It's easy to call this a tech problem. But the war isn't just external. It's inside you, too.

We've conditioned ourselves to fear boredom. To treat silence like a failure state. Stillness feels unproductive, even though that's where the best thinking begins. You don't get clarity from scanning ten hot takes. You get it by staying with ambiguity long enough to let coherence emerge.

This is the trap: when novelty becomes your baseline, clarity feels too slow to be useful. You start to avoid the very conditions that produce it.

Reclaiming your attention isn't a lifestyle tweak. It's an act of rebellion—a conscious refusal to be a product in someone else's system.

This doesn't mean disappearing from the world. It means designing friction where you need resistance, and flow where you need focus. Ask yourself: "What am I giving my attention to, and what is it doing to me?" Then build your space, tools, and time around that question.

Attention is like water. Left uncontained, it floods aimlessly. But when directed, it sculpts. It nourishes. It powers. Your job is to build the channel, daily, imperfectly, deliberately.

You won't win the attention war with willpower alone. You need structure. You need boundaries. You need rituals that anchor you back to signal. Clarity is not the result of effort alone; it's the result of design.

This war isn't going anywhere. But it doesn't have to win.

The moment you notice the noise and choose not to follow it, you've already begun to take your mind back.

Clarity begins the moment you choose to aim your attention, *before someone else decides for you..*

Chapter 4: Emotional Static

If clarity were just about logic, we'd all be masters of it by now. We know how to reason, how to analyze, how to follow steps, and trace consequences. And yet, we still find ourselves confused, conflicted, or frozen at precisely the moments we most need to act with confidence. That's not a failure of intellect. It's the interference of emotion, less like a sudden storm, more like a constant hum that disrupts signal fidelity without us even noticing.

This is emotional static. Not emotion itself, but the *interference pattern* emotion creates when it's unmanaged, misread, or left unacknowledged.

There's a fundamental misunderstanding at the heart of modern thinking about emotion. We tend to fall into one of two traps. Either, we treat emotion as noise, irrational, distracting, something to be suppressed in favor of "rational" decision-making. Or we do the opposite, treating every feeling as sacred, as inherently meaningful, as if our emotions were always wise. Both positions distort clarity.

Emotion isn't the enemy of clarity. But it isn't clarity itself either. Emotion is **data**, powerful, fast-moving, and often fuzzy data. Like a weather system moving through your mind, it shapes what you see and how you respond. And like the weather, it changes constantly. If you don't learn to read it, track it, and contextualize it, it will blow you off course every time.

When you're sad, the future feels smaller. When you're angry, your threat detection systems go haywire. When you're ashamed, your brain tries to hide rather than solve. These aren't flaws, they're adaptive responses. But in a complex, high-stakes world where the consequences of misperception are steep, adaptive isn't always accurate. And what feels emotionally honest can often be strategically wrong.

This is the dilemma. Emotions carry truth, but not all the truth. They can point to something important, such as a violation of your boundaries, a signal that your values are being compromised, or a sense that something isn't right. But they can also lie. They can be echoes of old stories, unresolved wounds, or distorted interpretations based on incomplete information. If you treat every emotional reaction as a compass, you end up navigating by shadows.

The first step toward clarity is not ignoring your emotions but **disentangling** from them just enough to see what they're doing to your perception. That requires awareness. Not analysis, not immediate interpretation, just the simple act of noticing.

"I'm flooded."

"I'm numb."

"I'm interpreting everything through this lens of anxiety."

These observations don't fix anything on their own. But they do interrupt the loop. They create space. And in that space, clarity can begin to reassert itself.

There's a myth that clarity requires calm. We must reach some inner stillness before we can make wise decisions. But life doesn't wait for stillness. It throws emotion at us at the exact moment we're forced to choose. The trick isn't to eliminate emotion, it's to create **emotional transparency**. To feel what you feel without letting it fog the lens. To let emotion inform the frame, not define the frame.

Practically, this means asking better questions. Not "How do I stop feeling this way?" but "What might this feeling be trying to protect?" Not "What's wrong with me?" but "What fear is underneath this reaction?" And then: "Is that fear true? Is it relevant? Or is it an old pattern speaking louder than the moment deserves?"

You can't reason your way to clarity if you're still hiding from your emotional drivers. You have to be willing to look at the distortion honestly. To sit with the signal long enough to parse its source. Sometimes the static resolves. Sometimes it doesn't. But even when it lingers, you're no longer reacting unthinkingly. You're seeing the distortion for what it is, **a filter, not a fact**.

Emotional static also shows up in relationships. It occurs when a partner says something neutral, but you interpret it as judgment. When a colleague disagrees, you feel dismissed. When your self-criticism flares because a decision you made didn't land as hoped. In these moments, clarity doesn't mean you're unaffected. It means you know what part of your reaction is about *this* moment, and what part is a ghost from another one.

You cannot clean your mind without first understanding the residue it's carrying.

One of the most dangerous forms of emotional static is urgency. Not real urgency, but the *emotional experience* of urgency, manufactured, chronic, compulsive. You feel like you must decide now. Must answer now. Must react now. That urgency short-circuits your clarity, because clarity needs time. Not continuously hours or days, but at least the time to breathe. To remember who you are. To check your alignment before you leap.

Clarity doesn't always feel good. Sometimes it leads you straight into grief, or anger, or shame you've been avoiding. But it's honest. It clears the false narratives and makes space for decisions rooted in the whole picture, not just the loudest emotion in the room.

So, the task isn't to suppress. It's to interpret. To notice the static without becoming the static. To build the muscle that says, "This feeling is real, but it might not be true." And then, to move forward not in denial of what you feel, but in a conscious relationship with it.

Because the thinker who cannot name their emotions becomes a servant to them. But the thinker who can recognize the distortion regains control of the signal.

And clarity, above all else, is a signal.

Chapter 5: Information Poisoning

There was a time, not so long ago, when not knowing something meant you didn't know it. You might go days, weeks, even years, unaware of a piece of information, and the world still turns. There was no shame in it. No pressure to catch up. No expectation that you should be constantly attuned to every development in every domain of life. You knew what you needed to know, and the rest could wait.

That time is over.

Today, we are surrounded, no, submerged, in information. It flows faster than our brains can process, more widely than our social structures can contextualize, and more aggressively than our nervous systems can handle. We call it "content," but that's a euphemism. Most of what passes through our mental gates is not content in the meaningful sense. It's cognitive sludge: decontextualized, misaligned, and unfiltered. And it's not just overwhelming. It's **poisonous**.

Information poisoning doesn't mean being lied to, although lies play a role. It means being exposed to so much fragmented, misaligned, or emotionally manipulative data that your internal filtering system breaks down. You lose the ability to discern relevance, quality, or applicability. You start mistaking volume for value. And worst of all, you begin to internalize distorted signals as part of your worldview, until you no longer know what you think because everything you're feeling was planted by someone else.

The symptoms are subtle at first. You feel scattered. Unfocused. Anxious, but not sure why. Then comes the paralysis. The feeling that there's too much to respond to, too many truths to weigh, too many potential traps in every opinion. So you delay. You lurk. You hedge. You copy the language of those who sound confident and borrow the ideas of those who speak loudly. It's not that you've stopped thinking. It's that your thinking no longer feels **yours**.

This is the danger. Not just misinformation, but the erosion of intellectual sovereignty. When your signal is polluted long enough, your internal compass stops pointing in any direction. You don't just become confused. You become *reprogrammable*.

Why is this happening?

Because information is no longer something we seek with intention. It's something that seeks us. It arrives uninvited. It floods your inbox, your feed, your notifications. It masquerades as insight but behaves like addiction. You don't remember choosing to care about half the things that fill your head. You do it because the machine trained you to.

The algorithms behind your media diet don't optimize for clarity. They optimize for engagement. Engagement rewards outrage, novelty, simplicity, and tribal reinforcement. That means your informational inputs are subtly engineered to inflame rather than inform. To stimulate reaction, not reflection. To keep you scrolling, not thinking. Over time, this rewires your thresholds. You become more sensitive to emotional signals and less attuned to factual depth. You grow impatient with ambiguity. You seek confirmation rather than comprehension.

Even well-meaning content creators contribute to the problem. To stay visible, they simplify complexity into punchlines, collapse nuance into binaries, and package insight into hyper-palatable micro-doses. You consume ten "frameworks for success" and still don't know what to do with your life. You read fifteen summaries of a book you never actually sat with long enough to absorb. You are full and starving.

The tragedy of information poisoning isn't ignorance. It's malnourishment disguised as insight.

What do you do?

You build filters. Not firewalls, filters. You can't opt out of the information ecosystem entirely, and pretending you can only creates new blind spots. But you can design your intake with intention. You can become selective about what you allow in. And more importantly, you can learn to trace what a piece of information *does* to you before deciding whether to keep it.

Ask yourself:
- Did this expand or shrink my understanding?
- Did it make me feel more grounded, or more reactive?
- Is this something I can use to build, or just another thing to perform?

- Who benefits from me believing this?

Those aren't rhetorical questions. They are the basic hygiene of modern cognition.

You also have to re-learn how to sit with information that doesn't resolve immediately. Clarity doesn't always come fast. Sometimes it requires digestion. Synthesis. Silence. But the poisoned mind wants closure, not understanding. It wants to slap a label on something and move on. And so we get headlines instead of depth, identity instead of ideas, dogma instead of discernment.

The antidote is **disciplined curiosity**—a commitment to engage slowly. To verify. To contextualize. To reflect. That's not fashionable, and it won't win you algorithmic favor. But it will protect your inner lens.

You are what you consume. Not just physically, but mentally. The quality of your thinking is downstream of the quality of your inputs. If you drink muddy water, your insights will be cloudy. If you breathe in pollution, your perception will suffer. You can't achieve clarity while feeding your mind a diet of noise and distortion.

This is not a call for purity. It's a call for agency. For sovereignty over what enters your mental bloodstream.

The world will not stop producing toxic information. But you can stop drinking it by the gallon.

You don't need to shut the world out. You need to stop leaving the door open to everything.

Reflection: Clearing the Fog

Before clarity comes, we have to name the fog.
- ∞ What kinds of mental "fog" do you recognize most often in your life? (e.g., overwhelm, people-pleasing, emotional static, decision fatigue)
- ∞ What external inputs most often cloud your thinking, and how do you usually respond to them?
- ∞ Can you identify one recurring thought or belief that might be *noise*, not signal?

You don't need to fix anything yet—just notice.
Awareness is the first filter.

Part II, Building Clean Thinking

Chapter 6: The Architecture of Insight

Clarity, when pursued intensely, always arrives at a paradox: we chase insight like it's a moment, a lightning strike, something sudden and dramatic. But real insight, the kind that changes how we think, not just what we believe, isn't sudden at all. It is built. Quietly. Repetitively. Often under pressure. Not in a flash of genius, but in the daily friction of pattern recognition, contradiction, and reflection. It isn't found. It's constructed. And the construction site is your mind.

This means that if you're serious about becoming someone who thinks clearly, you'll have to let go of the fantasy that insight arrives. The truth is, it requires somewhere to land. A structure. A scaffolding. An internal architecture that can hold the weight of what's been realized without collapsing under it. Insight alone is not enough. What matters is whether you've done the deeper work, laid the foundation, reinforced the frame, and made space for it to live.

This is where most people stall. They feel the flicker of a breakthrough, but because there's no system beneath it, it floats away. They collect insights the way others collect inspirational quotes, momentarily charged, quickly forgotten. But insight that is not metabolized becomes noise. And over time, the more noise you gather in the name of inspiration, the harder it becomes to access absolute clarity.

Eventually, you learn to stop romanticizing the moment of breakthrough. You begin to understand that insight is less like a revelation and more like a revision, a slow reshaping of your internal model until it reflects the truth with more accuracy and less effort. You stop chasing genius and start committing to structure. You begin to refine how you think, not just what you notice. You calibrate your mind to detect signals more quickly and hold them longer.

This is what the architecture of insight looks like in practice: You return to unresolved questions rather than rushing to answers. You build reflective muscle, so your thoughts have space to unfold. You treat tension as a forge, not a failure. You stop avoiding contradiction and begin using it to triangulate what's real. You start to see that insight emerges not despite ambiguity, but because of it.

There is no shortcut for this. You don't get to skip the scaffolding stage just because you've had a strong reaction or an elegant idea. Every insight must be translated into something usable: an operating principle, a better question, a refined filter. It must be integrated, not just admired. If you don't build it into your system, whatever that system is, then it won't hold. Insight is not self-reinforcing. It must be reinforced by action, tested in tension, and embedded in habits that shape future perception.

It's uncomfortable at first, this transition from romanticizing insight to architecting it. It strips away the dopamine of novelty. But in exchange, you gain something far more durable: grounded clarity. The kind that doesn't collapse when the wind changes. The type that survives emotional turbulence. The kind that makes future insights easier to recognize, because you've cleared a space for them to arrive.

This shift changes your identity. You no longer think of yourself as someone who occasionally has good ideas. You become someone who maintains the structure where good ideas can take root. You're not the source of the signal. You're the builder of the lens that catches it. And that lens, if maintained, sharpens over time. It makes you more precise. Less reactive. More resilient. Not because you know more, but because you've learned how to hold what you already know more cleanly.

That's what clarity ultimately is: a house your mind can live in without collapsing every time reality changes. It's not fragile. It's not brittle. It's adaptive, but stable. Flexible, but grounded. A structure that can hold new truths without needing to be rebuilt from scratch every time something unexpected arrives.

Clarity isn't built in moments of brilliance; it's built in the moments you return to your structure when brilliance fades.

Chapter 7: The Bias Layer

Before a single thought arrives, before a word forms in your head, before your brain kicks into conscious analysis, your system has already made a judgment. It has already been filtered, distorted, emphasized, and ignored. This happens so fast, so instinctively, that we don't even notice it. We assume our thoughts arise from reality. But often, they arise from *our relationship to reality*, a relationship shaped by deep, unconscious bias.

Clarity doesn't begin with better thoughts. It starts with noticing what warps the space those thoughts arise in. This is the bias layer. And if you don't confront it, you'll spend your life polishing the glass while ignoring the distortion in the lens itself.

Bias, in this context, isn't about politics or prejudice in the social sense. It's about **cognitive shape**, the invisible contours of how we interpret information, assign meaning, and protect identity. We all carry a constellation of biases, inherited from biology, culture, trauma, habits, and past survival strategies. They aren't chosen. But they *do* become automated. And automation, unchecked, becomes a constraint.

The danger isn't in having biases. It's in treating them as truth.

Bias is the first filter through which reality is passed. It tells your system what to notice, what to amplify, and what to reject. It whispers, "This confirms what you already believe. This contradicts it; be suspicious. This feels familiar, trust it. This feels strange, dismiss it." And if you're not aware this is happening, clarity becomes nearly impossible. Because what you think is clean thinking is often just *reinforced distortion*.

One of the most insidious aspects of bias is that it hides behind fluency. When something feels *intuitively true*, that doesn't mean it's true. It usually means it fits your existing frame. It doesn't create friction. It doesn't require reconfiguration. So your system accepts it, and then rewards you for your "insight." You feel sharp. Aligned. Even virtuous. But what you've done is looped back into confirmation.

This is why insight often comes from friction, not fluency. The sharpest revelations rarely feel comfortable. They feel irritating, humbling, and disorienting because they're bumping into a part of your map you didn't know was there.

To build absolute clarity, you have to get curious about your friction points. Do not avoid them. Do not override them. Do not therapize them away. But *examine* them. Ask: What am I resisting here? Why? What belief is being protected by that resistance?

Bias is not just a cognitive pattern. It's an *emotional bodyguard* for identity. If you've built your sense of self around being independent, your bias will screen out signals that point to your need for support. If you were raised to value certainty, your bias will reject ambiguity before it even registers. If you've been rewarded for being right, your bias will contort evidence to avoid any sign that you were wrong.

This means clarity doesn't just threaten your thinking. It threatens your narrative. And that's why it's so hard to maintain. Because to clean your thinking, you often have to grieve part of who you've been.

There's no hack for this. No shortcut to self-neutrality. But there is practice.

It begins with noticing patterns in your emotional responses. Clarity often hides behind overreactions. When something makes you disproportionately angry, afraid, or defensive, it's likely not about the event itself. It's about what that event *means* inside your preloaded bias script.

Start there. Don't ask, "Why is this situation so irrational?" Ask, "What bias is being challenged by this?" That question does something radical; it interrupts the script. It creates a space between trigger and interpretation. And in that space, clean thinking can begin.

Another path is to examine what you've *never* questioned. Often, our most influential biases are embedded not in what we obsess about, but in what we take as self-evident. These are the "of course" beliefs. Of course, people are selfish. Of course, success means growth. Of course, rest is laziness. These are the axioms that have never been tested because they're buried so deep they feel like the floor.

But what if they're not the floor? What if they're just early wallpaper?

As you begin to peel back the layers, the house of self-perception becomes noisier. That's expected. Bias, when confronted, resists. It whispers, "This work isn't productive." It says, "You're overcomplicating things." It recruits urgency, shame, and logic to maintain its integrity.

This is the emotional economy of distortion. Bias protects the short-term self from long-term discomfort. But clarity asks you to reverse that contract. To absorb some discomfort now in exchange for future coherence. To endure the awkwardness of dissonance in the service of building a cleaner lens.

This doesn't mean erasing all bias. That's a myth. Your nervous system will always prioritize specific cues. Your memory will always lean toward stories that kept you safe. But you *can* build a conscious relationship with your bias layer. You can track it. You can check its work. You can treat every strong opinion, every snap judgment, every easy certainty as a data point, not a verdict.

And over time, you'll find that clarity begins to arise with less friction. Not because your mind is free of distortion, but because it's no longer enslaved by it. You see your biases as *actors*, not *authors*. You factor them into your process instead of letting them define your conclusions.

That shift is everything.

Because once you understand how your bias layer works, you stop mistaking **certainty for clarity**. You stop mistaking **resonance for truth**. And you begin to hold your thinking, not as something sacred, but as something iterative, evolving, and incomplete.

That humility doesn't make you indecisive. It makes you *dangerously precise*. Because now, your decisions are built not on identity defense, but on actual contact with the world as it is.

Clean perception requires clean permission: to change your mind. To notice when you're wrong. To learn without shame. To stand still in ambiguity without collapsing into premature knowing.

This is what lives beneath the clarity you see on the surface. Not superior logic. Not perfect objectivity. But a *relentless willingness* to examine the distortions that live at the edge of your perception.

That's the bias layer. And when you learn to see through it, not erase it, but *see through it*, your whole way of thinking shifts.

You don't just think more clearly.

You *become someone your mind can trust*.

Chapter 8: Mental Hygiene

We understand hygiene in the physical sense. We shower, brush, disinfect, and sanitize not because we're dirty people, but because we know what happens when small accumulations go unchecked. A bit of grit today, a bit of oil tomorrow, left long enough, it becomes rot. Breakdown. Infection. Nobody questions the logic. Cleanliness is not about perfection. It's about **maintenance**.

But when it comes to the mind, we forget this entirely. We imagine that clarity should show up when we need it, untainted, fully intact, ready to perform on demand. And when it doesn't, we assume we've failed. We don't consider that clarity is subject to contamination. That thought, like skin or teeth or muscle, requires care, not just in crisis, but in rhythm.

This is the quiet discipline of **mental hygiene**. It's not glamorous. It doesn't trend. It doesn't offer immediate dopamine. But it is the invisible scaffolding behind every clear thinker you've ever admired. Not just what they know, but how they preserve the **internal conditions that let them see clearly when others panic**.

Let's be honest. Most of us don't clean our minds; we cram more in. We consume, absorb, scroll, listen, react. And then we wonder why we're foggy, why the brain feels gummed up. Why decisions come slowly or not at all, it's not a lack of capacity. It's **mental congestion**, too many unresolved fragments, emotional leftovers, and thought loops all competing for processing power.

Clarity doesn't die from confusion. It dies from accumulation.

Just like you don't notice how dirty your windows are until sunlight hits them, you don't see how foggy your mind has become until a moment of silence lands, and suddenly you feel uneasy. You reach for your phone. You turn on the music. You interrupt your stillness. That discomfort isn't boredom. It's a backlog. It's the mental residue you've been avoiding, the emotional static, the half-made decisions, the unprocessed events that are quietly coating your lens.

Mental hygiene starts with **acknowledgment**: not that you're broken, but that your mind, like your body, lives in a world full of contaminants. Every input has a cost. Every unresolved interaction has a footprint. You don't have to fear that, but you do have to respect it.

So what does mental hygiene look like in practice?

It begins with **intentional clearing**. This isn't the same as distraction. Distraction numbs. Clearing reveals. That might mean daily reflection. It might mean writing, not for an audience, not even for insight, but to *move the internal clutter somewhere else*. Thoughts that stay in your head tend to distort. Thoughts that are put on paper tend to quiet down. It's not magic. It's physics. You offload. You release.

But clearing alone isn't enough. You also need **containment**. Your mind is not meant to be always-on, always-available, always open to interruption. The thinker who never sets boundaries around their mental energy becomes porous. And porous minds don't think, they **leak**.

Containment means setting rituals. The time when you don't engage. Places where you don't process. Devices that are put away, not because you're anti-tech, but because you're pro-clarity. Mental hygiene is not asceticism. It's curation. It's the conscious decision to gatekeep your consciousness.

And then, there's the emotional layer. One of the least-discussed pollutants in a thinker's mind is **emotional residue** from unresolved interactions. The argument you didn't finish. The email that still stings. The apology you owe but haven't made. We act like these things fade with time. But they don't. They calcify. They harden into emotional plaque. And just like physical plaque, it's not always visible, but it degrades the system from within.

If you've ever had a day when you couldn't focus, couldn't write, couldn't get clarity no matter how hard you tried, ask yourself: What am I holding onto that I haven't named? What emotional knots are pulling against my thinking? What loops are still open?

Mental hygiene isn't about constant self-analysis. It's about **closure**. When something is unfinished, it stays alive in your cognitive bandwidth. That doesn't mean you can resolve everything. But it does mean you can stop pretending unresolved things don't have a cost. You can create small rituals of completion. Even writing "I don't have an answer yet" can be a closing move, an acknowledgment that the loop exists, and that for now, it's paused.

There's also a social dimension to this. Who you spend time with, what voices you absorb, what emotional tone you marinate in, these things seep in whether you choose them or not. Mental hygiene sometimes means **emotional distancing** from people who don't take responsibility for their mental state. Clarity cannot thrive in a field of projection and volatility.

This doesn't make you cold. It makes you strategic. If your mind is your instrument, you must protect its tuning.

Finally, there's the hygiene of **expectation**. Many thinkers destroy their clarity by holding themselves to impossible cognitive standards. They expect insight on demand. They expect constant emotional neutrality. They wish to produce peak focus every day. These expectations don't elevate your thinking. They contaminate it. Because when reality doesn't meet them, shame creeps in. And shame, once embedded, becomes the dirtiest filter of all.

You don't need a perfect mind. You need a **well-kept one**. You need space between thoughts. You need intentional emotional recycling. You need time to zoom out. You need moments where your only job is to clean the lens, not produce brilliance through it.

Think of this book not just as a manual for better thought, but as a **maintenance schedule**. Each chapter is a different part of the system you're learning to tend. Each reflection is a wipe of the glass. You're not building a fortress. You're cultivating a greenhouse. One where clarity can thrive, not because you're constantly achieving, but because you've learned how to preserve the conditions it needs to grow.

Mental hygiene won't win you applause. But it will help you regain control of your mind.

And in this world, that might be the most radical achievement of all.

Chapter 9: Filters, Not Funnels

In a world designed to overwhelm you, clarity doesn't come from openness. It comes from filtration. We've been taught to think of filters as limitations, as restrictions that narrow possibilities. But in reality, filters are the only reason you can think at all. Without them, you become a funnel, open to everything, anchored to nothing. You absorb input indiscriminately, and eventually, you drown in it.

Most people don't realize they've become funnels. They scroll, they skim, they consume without asking why. They confuse exposure for discernment, access for agency. It feels productive because they're learning something new, or staying "informed." But none of it integrates. None of it sticks. Their signal is buried under the weight of what was never meant for them in the first place.

The real thinkers, the ones who produce clarity in complexity, do something different. They filter. Ruthlessly. Not because they're closed-minded, but because they know their mind is a finite resource. They understand that discernment isn't about snobbery. It's about survival. In an era of infinite content, filtering is not a constraint. It's a lifeline.

To filter well, you need structure. Not just personal taste or intuition, but a conscious system for selecting what enters your awareness. That system has three layers: **criteria**, **calibration**, and **cadence**.

Criteria is the first line of defense. It's the decision-making lens that defines what qualifies as a relevant signal. What kind of information aligns with your values, your goals, your current learning arc? If you haven't set these criteria deliberately, someone else's agenda will do it for you. The algorithm will decide what matters. The loudest voice in the room will steer your attention. Criteria don't have to be fixed, but they must be explicit. If you can't name what belongs, you won't notice what doesn't.

Then comes **calibration**, the ongoing refinement of what earns your bandwidth. You start to notice when you've let in too much, or the wrong type. You begin to feel the weight of consuming things that clutter instead of clarify. Calibration is where self-awareness sharpens. It's the feedback loop that helps you adjust, not just based on how much you're consuming, but how you feel afterward. Drained? Unsettled? Confused? That's not curiosity, it's cognitive smog. You learn to recognize that feeling, and to treat it as data.

Finally, there's **cadence**. This is about timing and rhythm. Even the right content, consumed at the wrong moment, can generate noise. Cadence is how you create space for absorption, integration, and recovery. It might mean checking the news once a week instead of every morning. It might mean limiting notifications to a single window in the day. It might mean reading one book deeply instead of ten summaries shallowly. Cadence is the pattern of attention that reinforces clarity instead of chasing novelty.

All three criteria, calibration and cadence, form a kind of mental hygiene. A way to protect your signal before it gets hijacked. And it's not just about what you consume. It applies to conversations, commitments, and even your internal dialogue. Filtering isn't limited to inputs. It's how you choose what to carry forward, what to revisit, what to let dissolve. It's how you reclaim sovereignty over your cognition.

This level of intentionality requires effort, especially at first. The world will not reward you for narrowing your focus. It will call you uninformed, out of touch, even selfish. But there's a quiet strength in knowing what's yours to carry. In holding a clean lens when everyone else is seeing through fog. In protecting your clarity, not with walls, but with wisdom.

And here's the more profound truth: filters don't isolate you. They make connections richer. When you've filtered out the static, you can engage with others from a place of presence instead of reactivity. You're not bringing your noise to the table; you're getting signal. You're not reacting to what you don't understand; you're responding to what matters.

So no, you don't need to become a funnel for the world's noise. You don't need to be endlessly available, endlessly absorbing, endlessly open. You need to be precise. You need to be sovereign. You need to guard your clarity like it's the foundation of every decision you'll make, because it is.

Clarity is not found at the bottom of a feed. It's built at the edge of attention. In a world addicted to input, the clearest minds will belong to those brave enough to *filter for what's truly theirs.*

Chapter 10: The Anti-Noise Protocol

Clarity is not a matter of accumulating more information. It's a matter of shedding distortion. And in a world that rewards loudness, friction, and frenzy, the most radical clarity often begins not with a decision, but with a refusal. A refusal to internalize what doesn't belong to you. A refusal to let your attention become collateral damage in someone else's storm.

This is the essence of the Anti-Noise Protocol.

It's not a checklist, a technique, or a productivity trick. It's a neurological stance—a kind of psychological posture you take, not against the world, but within it. The Anti-Noise Protocol begins the moment you stop treating interference as benign. Noise is more than just an inconvenience. It is a distortion. And distortion leads to drift, subtle at first, then systemic.

Noise wears many masks. Some of it is obvious: endless notifications, doomscrolling, the ambient hum of digital tension. But the more corrosive noise is internal. The kind that loops silently. Unfinished conversations you replay. Judgments you absorbed but never interrogated. Self-doubt disguised as prudence. This kind of noise is sneaky. It mimics thinking but produces only exhaustion. It drowns signal in a fog of subtle static.

Most people try to outwork noise. They push harder, focus longer, and grit their way through it. But friction isn't always a sign that you need more effort. Sometimes it's a sign that your signal has been compromised. The Anti-Noise Protocol begins here, with a different question. Not "How can I power through this?" but "What interference am I treating as signal?"

The first step is recognition. Noticing when you've taken on urgency that isn't yours. Identifying patterns of over-preparation, over-connection, or over-accommodation that quietly erode your focus. Most distortion doesn't come from chaos. It comes from unexamined agreement, subtle contracts you sign without realizing: to respond fast, to be agreeable, to always be available, to know everything, all the time.

The protocol invites a different rhythm. It begins with environmental design: creating spaces, digital, emotional, and physical, that reinforce your clarity baseline. For some, this means fewer tabs open. For others, it means stronger boundaries around interruptions, tighter filters on incoming requests, and cleaner relationships with input. You cannot metabolize contaminated information and expect pure thought on the other side.

But anti-noise isn't about isolation. It's about coherence. The ability to detect when your internal compass starts to tilt, not because you're weak, but because you're awake. Awake to the fact that sustained distortion has a cost: in time, in trust, in discernment. You don't always see that cost until later, when you're retrofitting clarity into decisions that should have never been made in fog.

And so the protocol deepens. It becomes a reflex to pause, not as evasion, but as calibration. You pause to ask: Am I thinking, or am I reacting? Am I responding to a signal or an echo? You pause not to disconnect, but to reclaim precision.

Eventually, the pause becomes a return—a return to mental sovereignty. The protocol doesn't demand perfection. It simply insists on return. The faster you return to the signal after you drift, the stronger your clarity muscle becomes. You stop chasing everything. You stop explaining everything. You begin to see how much time you spent decoding noise that had no meaning.

Over time, your appetite changes. You crave clean questions. Crisp conversations. Input that respects your cognition. You notice the difference between emotional turbulence and intellectual engagement. You no longer mistake noise for insight. And you no longer stay in rooms, physical or mental, where clarity has to fight for air.

People often misinterpret the Anti-Noise Protocol as a form of avoidance. But it's the opposite. It's radical engagement, with what's real, what's useful, what's yours. It doesn't make you rigid. It makes you precise. You don't cut people out. You cut the distortion out. You build a life where clarity doesn't have to be recovered; it's maintained.

Because once you've experienced what it's like to move through the world without interference, you don't want to go back. You don't want to explain your instincts to chaos. You don't want to waste your insight managing other people's urgency. You want a clean signal. And when you find it, you protect it, not out of fragility, but out of respect.

Noise will always exist. But it doesn't have to live in you.

And that is the heart of the Anti-Noise Protocol.

Chapter 11: Internal Signal Calibration

There is a quiet crisis in modern cognition, one that doesn't show up in headlines but erodes us from the inside out: we no longer trust our internal signals. We second-guess our instincts, outsource our judgment, and defer endlessly to experts, metrics, and algorithms. In doing so, we confuse precision with wisdom and validation with alignment. Clarity suffers not because we're uninformed, but because we're **disconnected from the feedback systems within ourselves**.

Internal signal calibration is the lost art of knowing what your body, mind, and intuition are trying to tell you, and learning how to distinguish between a signal and a surge.

Every system, human or mechanical, requires feedback. Without it, you can't correct the course. You can't adapt. You can't grow. But feedback is only valuable when you know how to read it, and only possible when the signal isn't buried beneath static.

The modern world doesn't just produce external noise. It breeds **internal confusion**, teaching us to distrust our gut. To ignore the tension in our shoulders. To override fatigue. To push through instinct in favor of expectation. But internal signals don't vanish when you ignore them. They reroute, first into anxiety, then into inertia, and eventually into collapse.

We misread the quiet signs:
The tightening in the chest after a meeting.
The restlessness that comes with working on a project that no longer fits.
The dull ache after agreeing to something we didn't mean.
The spike of adrenaline that hits just before we hit "publish" on something that doesn't feel true.

Each of these is a **signal**, not a symptom. But we've been trained to treat these moments as obstacles to overcome, not messages to interpret.

So how do you recalibrate?

You begin by listening differently. Not reactively. Not judgmentally. But diagnostically.

When you feel resistance, ask:
Is this a signal of misalignment, or just fear of exposure?
When you feel fatigue, ask:
Is this the cost of deep work, or the symptom of a fractured focus loop?
When you feel urgency, ask:
Is this real, or is it an emotional hijack dressed as strategy?
These aren't easy questions. And they don't always have clean answers. But they break the trance. They interrupt the pattern of override-and-regret that has replaced real reflection.

Calibration isn't just about intuition. It's about **discernment**. It's about building a map of your responses over time, so that when your stomach drops, or your mind fogs, or your energy vanishes, you know whether it's a red flag or just routine turbulence.

Start keeping a mental log. When you act on a signal and it leads somewhere good, note it. When you ignore a subtle cue and regret it, note that too. Over weeks and months, you'll start to rebuild a relational map of your cognition. You'll learn the difference between an old fear speaking and a new truth emerging. You'll know which doubts are worth pausing for, and which are just echoes of someone else's voice.

One of the great lies of performance culture is that hesitation equals weakness. But not all hesitation is fear. Some of it is **precision, trying to surface**. Some of it is your internal system flagging a mismatch between your words and your values, your strategy and your actual capacity, your identity and your environment.

This is internal friction. And while it's uncomfortable, it's also useful, if you listen.

Of course, internal signals aren't always accurate. That's where calibration becomes crucial. Not all instincts are aligned. Some are trauma responses, automated loops, outdated heuristics from another phase of life. The signal may be *real*, but not always *relevant*. That's why self-trust isn't enough. You need **self-verification**, a way of testing your signals against reality, not in a single moment, but across patterns.

That might mean journaling. It might mean feedback loops with people who know how to reflect without projecting. It might mean revisiting your decisions after the fact and asking not just "Was it right?" but "Was I clear when I made it?"

Calibration is less about certainty than **coherence**. Do your thoughts, feelings, and behaviors point in the same direction, or are they pulling you apart?

When they're aligned, clarity feels embodied. Decisions come not with fanfare but with quiet certainty. You know, without theatrics, that you're moving in the right direction, even if the path ahead is still murky. That's absolute clarity. Not controlled. Not omniscience. Just *integrity between signal and action.*

Let's not pretend this is easy. We live in a culture that rewards simulation, doing what looks right, sounds smart, or performs well on a stage. Internal clarity doesn't trend. It doesn't announce itself. It whispers. And only those who've tuned their filters can hear it.

So, the work isn't about finding a guru. It's about becoming your own.

Rebuilding the trust that was eroded by years of override. Relearning the difference between tension and trauma. Reawakening the sense of "off" that saved you once and can guide you again.

Internal signal calibration is how you reclaim agency in a world that wants to program you. It's how you stop being a reaction machine and become a decision-maker again. It's how you move from borrowed wisdom to embodied knowing.

It won't come overnight. But with each clear signal followed, each false signal corrected, you move closer to a mind you can trust.

And a mind you can trust is a mind that can see.

Chapter 12: The Signal Recovery Protocol

Clarity isn't something you acquire once and carry forever. It's something you recover, again and again, after the impact. After the failure. After the choice, you can't undo. After the meeting that shook your confidence, or the moment you realized you were listening to noise and calling it truth. The mind, no matter how trained, picks up static. It drifts. It misreads. It fills in gaps with familiar distortions. Which means the question is never whether you lose clarity. The question is whether you have a protocol for returning to it.

Recovery doesn't begin with analysis. It starts with honesty. Not intellectual honesty, but emotional. You have to be willing to look at what the moment extracts from you, your trust, your attention, your sense of control, and name the cost without flinching. That cost is real, even when the outcome was technically correct. Even when others call it a win, it's still a win. Because clarity has an emotional load, and if you don't name it, you carry it forward unexamined. You start making decisions with less heart. Less risk tolerance. Less belief in yourself.

That's why ritualized reflection matters. Not because it's indulgent, but because it's preventative. It's how you recover the signal, not by dwelling on the past, but by creating a space wide enough actually to hear it. You sit with the decision, not as a judge, but as a translator. What was I trying to protect? Where did I override my instinct? What did I pretend not to notice? These are not casual questions. They're a form of self-calibration. A diagnostic for distortion. A way to catch when your perception gets warped by urgency, emotion, or fear, and to tune it back toward reality.

And it's not just about identifying errors. It's about re-establishing coherence. You're not auditing outcomes to validate yourself. You're reverse-engineering moments to understand your thinking. To see how it behaved under pressure. To study the shape of your clarity when it was threatened. That pattern is everything. Because once you understand it, you can work with it. You can train for it. You can build architecture around it, structures that help you stay clearer, longer.

But clarity isn't restored by insight alone. Insight is the first step. Integration is the second. You have to live what you've seen. Embed it. Use it. That might mean rewriting your decision-making protocols. It might mean journaling not what you did, but how you thought. It might mean having the complicated conversation you postponed, now with more awareness and less armor. Without integration, reflection is performance. It gives the illusion of clarity, without the consequence.

This is the heart of the signal recovery protocol: not recovery as reversion, but as revision. You don't bounce back. You return differently. And if the practice is deep enough, you return better. Not because the failure didn't cost you, but because you mined it. You metabolized it. You let it refine the very system through which you perceive the world.

Sometimes the loop you're closing isn't intellectual. It's emotional. A rupture in trust. A moment of misalignment that scraped something invisible and raw. You don't restore signal there by doubling down on logic. You do it by acknowledging the bruise without retreating from the touch. You name the ache, and in naming it, you stop letting it speak in disguise, through avoidance, aggression, or self-doubt.

In practice, this might look like less drama and more debrief. You ask what worked and what didn't, not as a performance, but as a muscle. You do it after the big decisions, but also after the subtle ones, after the choice to speak up. After the moment you held back. You notice not just what happened, but how it felt to navigate. What pulled your attention? What you resisted. Where were you when you collapsed? This is how you clean your lens, not once, but habitually.

It doesn't take long. Ten minutes. Sometimes less. But the return compounds. You begin to know yourself in tension. You begin to see patterns before they harden. You start to make decisions from the version of you that's more whole, not just more efficient. And over time, that changes everything, not just how you choose, but how you recover when your choices cost you.

Most of us don't suffer from a lack of intelligence. We suffer from incomplete loops. Half-heard instincts. Unfinished reflections. Noise is mistaken for insight because we never gave it the time to sort itself out. That's what the signal recovery protocol protects against. It's not just a thinking tool. It's a clarity ritual. One that treats your perception as sacred, worth cleaning, worth restoring, worth listening to again.

Because clarity will falter, that's not a flaw. That's the nature of being awake in a noisy world. The goal isn't to become invincible. The goal is to become someone who can return. Someone who can clean their field. Someone who can ask the hard questions without collapsing under the weight of the answers.

That's how clarity becomes a way of life, not through perfection, but through recovery, not through brilliance, but through discipline. You lose the signal. You return to it. You clean the channel. You continue.

The signal gets lost. The work is to return to yourself, to clarity, to a signal you can trust again.

Chapter 13: Embodied Clarity

You can't think your way into clarity and expect it to hold if your body remains in chaos. This is one of the most neglected truths in modern life, especially among high-functioning thinkers. We tend to over-index on the cognitive, believing clarity is purely about better analysis, sharper logic, and cleaner frameworks. But what happens when your nervous system is dysregulated? When your sleep is fractured, your breathing is shallow, and your posture is collapsed. No thought model in the world can override a body that's still bracing for impact.

That's where embodied clarity begins, not with ideas, but with sensation. With a willingness to treat the body not as a vessel to carry the mind, but as the first instrument that registers signal and distortion alike. A body can tell the truth before the mind catches up. But only if we're trained to listen.

Here's the paradox: people who seek clarity often do so precisely because they don't feel safe. Uncertainty, overwhelm, and noise are not abstract states. They're physiological. We feel them in our gut, our jaw, our shoulders. We tighten. We brace. We collapse inward or lash outward. The internal noise isn't just cognitive; it's somatic. And yet we rarely build practices that treat the body as part of the clarity equation.

When your body is holding tension, you can't think straight. But more subtly, you begin to doubt yourself. You confuse urgency with importance. You interpret your physiological arousal as a sign that something's wrong when it might just be that you haven't exhaled all day. This is why so many well-meaning thinkers spiral into loops of over-analysis. Not because they lack intelligence, but because they've disconnected their thinking from their sensing. They're trying to pilot a jet with no instruments. They're flying blind, inside themselves.

Embodied clarity isn't about adopting a "wellness routine." It's not about smoothies and stretching. It's about integrating your perception. Recognizing that what your body registers matters, and that ignoring it isn't stoicism, it's self-sabotage. You can't cultivate strategic calm if your body's been trained to interpret stillness as danger.

That's what trauma does, on micro or macro scales. It rewires your relationship to quiet. It can make the signal feel unfamiliar, even threatening. Which is why so many people chase stimulation, noise, and drama: it feels more predictable than the stillness they can't trust. They mistake peace for boredom. Clarity for detachment. Safety for stagnation. And they sabotage the very environments that would allow them to hear themselves again.

The antidote is slow reconnection. Not intellectual insight, but somatic re-attunement. You start by noticing where your body clenches during challenging conversations, where you shrink when you're dismissed. Where you override hunger, fatigue, instinct, because someone told you to. You begin to rebuild trust by listening differently. Not just to words, but to breath. Not just to reactions, but to posture. You let your body teach you what's true, and what's just a habit of fear.

And as you build that awareness, something strange begins to happen: you stop needing to perform clarity. You don't need to over-explain yourself, because you're rooted in something more profound than logic. You don't need to dominate a conversation to feel solid. You're not clarity-as-aesthetic. You're clarity-as-presence. And people think that. They trust it, not because you have all the answers, but because you're not abandoning yourself in search of them.

Leaders who operate this way change rooms, not through charisma, but through coherence. They don't flinch when others are reactive. They don't default to control when tension rises. Their nervous system becomes the metronome for the group, a steady pulse of unforced presence. This is not magic. It's a regulation. And it's trainable.

If you want to think clearly in a messy world, you cannot ignore systems thinking. That system is you, flesh and blood, breath and tension, impulse and stillness. It's not just your ideas that need hygiene. It's your state. And when you build clarity into the body, not just the brain, you become less manipulable, less reactive, and more sovereign.

Embodied clarity doesn't just help you think better, it brings you back to the wisdom your body never forgot.

Chapter 14: Clarity-Led Systems

Most people think of systems as sterile. Boring. Mechanical. Something you build once and forget about. But systems, when constructed properly, are the architecture of clarity. They are the skeletal structure behind sustainable insight. And in a world where the pace of change is high and attention is low, clarity that doesn't live in your environment won't live for long.

To live cleanly, you cannot rely on memory, motivation, or momentary insight. You need scaffolding, external, intentional structures that hold your signal when your mind is overwhelmed, tired, or hijacked by emotion. Systems are how we protect our best thinking from the entropy of the everyday. They are how we embed discernment into the default.

A clarity-led system isn't just efficient. It's expressive. It says something about what matters. It doesn't just execute; it reinforces the conditions under which right action is most likely to emerge. The purpose of such a system isn't to constrain, it's to clarify. Not to override judgment, but to sharpen it. And if it's doing its job well, it should make intelligent behavior easier, not harder.

This is where most systems fall apart. They become bureaucratic instead of supportive. They fossilize insights instead of evolving them. Someone has one brilliant thought in 2017, writes it into a policy, and then enshrines it for the next decade, even after the conditions that justified it no longer exist. That's not a clarity-led system. That's an ossified one. And it usually indicates that the real thinking stopped long ago.

True clarity-led systems behave more like living documents than rigid commandments. They get reviewed, tested, and pruned. Their edges shift as your understanding does. They are designed for feedback, for friction, even for failure, because a system that doesn't let error surface will eventually conceal its breakdown. In high-trust environments, this kind of system becomes a mirror, not a mask. It shows you where your clarity is slipping before your performance does.

But there's a deeper function as well. When you build systems that encode clarity, you also protect yourself from being seduced by your past confusion. It's easy, in the middle of chaos, to forget what you once knew clearly. It's easy to revert to old behaviors, outdated metrics, or compromised decisions under pressure. Systems that are clarity-led create an archive of your cleanest thinking, snapshots of what mattered when you weren't under duress.

The most powerful systems aren't complex; they're unambiguous. A simple "one-touch rule" that says: If I touch it, I finish it. A reflection prompt that auto-triggers every Friday, asking: What signals did I miss this week? A client onboarding doc that doesn't just list deliverables but articulates the values behind them. These are small interventions. But their cumulative effect is profound. They offload ambiguity. They return attention to the signal. They raise the floor of performance.

And when that becomes habitual, when your daily life is surrounded by systems that reinforce what's real, what matters, what works, you begin to notice something strange: clarity becomes quieter. It stops requiring heroic focus. It stops being this sacred thing you have to fight to access. It's just… there. Present in the background. Embedded into how you act, not just how you think.

This is not about perfection. Every system degrades over time. Conditions shift. New tensions emerge. But the hallmark of a clarity-led system isn't that it lasts forever. It prompts re-evaluation. It knows when to fade. It retires itself when no longer needed. It trusts that the clarity it was built on will find a new form if it's no longer the right one.

When you walk into a clarity-led system, you feel it. There's a tone—a rhythm. Decisions don't feel arbitrary. Confusion is surfaced, not shamed. Reflection is operationalized, not outsourced. And above all, there is a shared confidence, not that everything will go right, but that when it doesn't, the system will help you make sense of why.

Many people live in systems that confuse them. Overcomplicated project tools, values statements no one believes in, KPIs that contradict each other, meetings where no one knows why they're there. These aren't just annoying. They're corruptive. They warp thinking. They pull people away from ownership and into survival. A system that punishes truth, that rewards conformity, that obscures responsibility, is not a system worth saving.

To build clarity-led systems, you must first ask a tricky question: What am I optimizing for? Not just in theory, but in everyday life. Am I building for ease or insight? For growth or image? For alignment or control? The answer to that question determines the shape of your systems. And you can't fake it. Your system will tell the truth even if you don't.

This is the real reason clarity-led systems matter. Not because they automate work. But because they reveal orientation. They show what you believe, not just what you say. They codify values into practice. They translate aspiration into form. And in doing so, they allow other people, not just you, to navigate reality with more integrity and less noise.

A sound system doesn't just scale your impact. It scales your clarity. And in a world addicted to complication, that's a radical act.

Chapter 15: Clear Communication Loops

Clean thinking isn't sustainable if it exists in isolation. You might reach a moment of insight alone, a flash of internal alignment, a private clarity. But the second you bring that insight into the world, it enters a feedback system. It meets the gaze, judgment, misunderstanding, or support of another human. And in that moment, your clarity becomes vulnerable to distortion, not just from their reaction, but from *how you interpret that reaction*.

This is why communication isn't just about transmitting thoughts. It's about **preserving clarity through signal loops**. And most loops are broken.

In everyday life, feedback is rarely clean. We speak through filters of culture, shame, expectation, and insecurity. We listen through noise, of assumptions, past wounds, and performative attention. The loop becomes corrupted. Meaning becomes mismatched. And the thinker, despite their best effort, ends up doubting their clarity, not because it was flawed, but because it was **unseen**.

This is the unspoken tragedy of many smart, perceptive people: they don't lose their clarity. They *stop trusting it* because it failed to gain the trust of others. The loop didn't complete, and in that vacuum, distortion returned.

A clear communication loop is not just about saying something accurately. It's receiving signal back in a way that *reinforces, refines, or respectfully challenges* that clarity. And if you don't design your life for those kinds of loops, your clarity will remain fragile. Beautiful in solitude. Brittle in contact.

Let's be clear: most communication systems are not built for clarity. They're built for speed, performance, hierarchy, and emotional safety. Truth in those systems becomes secondary to coherence and comfort. People signal what's acceptable, not what's real. They offer agreement to avoid conflict or critique to assert dominance. And in that haze, the original clarity gets buried under emotional sediment.

To maintain clean thinking in this fog, you need to **cultivate feedback environments that are signal-sensitive**. That means building loops with people who know how to receive clarity without distorting it through their own needs. People who can hold your truth without editing it through their bias. People who offer you their perception without assuming it should replace yours.

These people are rare. But they are not mythical. You find them by becoming one. You attract clarity-sensitive communicators by practicing **clean mirroring**, the ability to reflect what you're hearing without projection. That means listening for meaning, not identity, and asking, not assuming. Slowing the loop, not closing it prematurely.

A clean communication loop has three phases: **transmit, reflect, and refine**.

You transmit your signal, what you see, believe, or feel, with as little distortion as possible. Not defensively. Not manipulatively. Just honestly, with awareness of your filters.

The listener then reflects, through questions, silence, body language, or summary. Their job isn't to agree. It's to **confirm they received the shape of what you meant**, not just the words you used. If they can't, the loop fails. Not because they're wrong, but because clarity didn't arrive.

Then comes refinement. Together, you re-express, re-listen, and slowly build a shared frame, not necessarily a shared belief, but a shared *understanding* of what is being communicated. That understanding is the loop. That is where clarity becomes relational, and therefore, resilient.

But most people never make it past phase one. They speak. They don't check for distortion. They move on. And over time, this trains the mind to expect **feedback blindness**. You stop looking for reflection. You internalize the distortion. You think, *maybe I'm just hard to understand.* Or worse, *perhaps I'm wrong for seeing it this way at all.*

That internalized static is corrosive. It doesn't just affect how you speak. It affects how you think. You begin to pre-edit your clarity to avoid confusion. You start shrinking your insight to make it palatable. You start abandoning your signal, not because you lost it, but because the world didn't echo it back.

And that's the risk of broken loops.

So, what's the antidote?

You build loops intentionally. You identify the people in your life who *listen*, not just hear. You notice who asks questions that sharpen your thinking instead of flattening it. You remember what it felt like the last time someone understood you *without translation*. And you feed those loops. You invest in them. You tell those people, "That helped me see more clearly." And then you do the same for them.

You also audit your reactive loops. Where do you rush to fill the silence? Where do you shut down when someone doesn't reflect agreement? Where do you interpret neutral feedback as rejection? These habits warp the loop before it completes.

At some point, if you're serious about clarity, not as a concept but as a way of being, you realize it's not just about how well you think. It's about how well your thinking lands. The signal in your mind, no matter how clean, doesn't complete itself in isolation. It needs contact. It needs reflection. Without that, you risk mistaking articulation for arrival. You assume that because you said it clearly in your head, it was received that way out loud. But that's rarely the case. Human communication is messy. Attention is fragmented. Meaning gets bent in transmission. So, if you want your clarity to endure, you have to build in the discipline of loop honesty.

Loop honesty is not a performance. It's not the clever use of interpersonal scripts. It's a relational hygiene that keeps the signal from degrading mid-transit. It sounds simple, "Can you reflect what you heard?" or "I'm not sure that landed, let me try again", but those questions carry weight. They are acts of responsibility. They acknowledge that clarity isn't one-sided. It's not enough to send a clean signal. You have to make sure it completes the loop. And you do that not through force, but through curiosity. You check. You clarify. Not because you doubt yourself, but because you respect the process enough not to leave it unfinished.

And it's in those honest loops, those small moments of checking, adjusting, asking for feedback, that your thinking sharpens. Not weakens. Because when you give others the chance to reflect on your words, they often return them with something you didn't see. A layer you missed. An emotional undertone you hadn't considered. A question that makes your original thought more dimensional, more robust. The insight doesn't get diluted. It gets refined. That's the quiet power of completing the loop: it makes clarity stronger than it was in your head.

But this only works when you're willing to prioritize signal over ego. When you stop treating correction as critique and start seeing it as collaboration, in that space, clarity is no longer just yours to protect. It becomes something that grows between people. And that growth, over time, begins to shape the environment around you. You stop tolerating conversations that trail off into misunderstanding. You stop pretending you understood when you didn't. You start modeling what it looks like to finish a thought, to ground a truth, to ask for resonance instead of approval.

And others respond. Not always immediately. But eventually, they mirror what they see in you. They slow down. They clarify. They reflect. The room shifts. The quality of interaction shifts. People start to reach not just for words, but for accuracy. They listen to understand, not to respond. And that feedback loop, once rare, becomes your default mode of communication.

That's the part of clarity we often overlook. We think of it as a solitary pursuit, an internal discipline. But its most transformative aspect is social. It creates a ripple. When you insist on clean loops, on finishing thoughts, checking resonance, refining meaning, you teach others to do the same. Without preaching. Without pushing. Just by doing it.

Clarity, then, becomes more than a mental asset. It becomes an environmental catalyst. It doesn't just help you think better; it teaches the people around you how to feel better, too. Not perfectly. Not always. But more often. And more generously. And in a noisy world, that is nothing short of revolutionary.

Chapter 16: The Long-Term View is the Clear View

There's a peculiar clarity that arises when you stretch your time horizon. It doesn't come from knowing more. It comes from seeing differently. When you step back far enough, the noise that once demanded your reaction fades into context. The emotional urgency that dominated your day loses its grip. You begin to perceive what's durable instead of what's dramatic. And in that space, a new kind of decision-making becomes possible, not just reactive or responsive, but rooted.

But stretching your time horizon isn't a passive shift. It requires effort. We are not wired for long-term clarity. Biologically, we're built for survival. Neurologically, we're biased toward immediacy. Socially, we are rewarded for speed and punished for pause. Everything around us reinforces the myth that thinking long means thinking later. But it doesn't. It means thinking now, through a different lens.

That lens is what distinguishes strategic clarity from tactical cleverness. It's what separates noise chasers from signal builders. Because the short view often feels clearer, it's closer, louder, and more measurable. But it's also deceptive. It pulls you into optimizing for metrics that won't matter in five years, building reputations you don't want to maintain, and chasing relevance in rooms you'll one day want to leave. The long-term view forces a reckoning not just with what's urgent, but with what's true.

That reckoning begins with uncomfortable questions. If I keep doing what I'm doing, who will I become? If my current pace continues, what part of me will burn out first: my body, my mind, or my values? If I achieve my goals but lose signal in the process, was it clarity or just momentum? These are not abstract concerns. They are the compass points of long-view clarity. They strip away the distractions that masquerade as progress and reveal what your trajectory holds.

And clarity at that scale demands courage. Because when you take the long view, you will look out of step. You will resist what others rush into. You will prioritize things that often go unnoticed, such as rest, reputation, relationship quality, or intellectual integrity. You will be mocked for your slowness and misunderstood for your discipline. And you must be okay with that because the clarity you are building is not designed to win this cycle. It is designed to endure.

This endurance is not just mental; it is systemic. Long-term clarity changes what you track. It reshapes how you build. You stop designing systems that max out your capacity and start creating ones that protect your future capacity. You begin to value sustainability over scale. You invest in redundancies, not as inefficiencies, but as lifelines. You let go of optimization as the highest goal and embrace resilience as the higher one. You build for what's next, not just what's now.

And as you do, something remarkable happens: you regain trust in your timing. You stop measuring your progress by how fast it's happening and start measuring by how aligned it feels. You start turning down opportunities that distort your direction. You begin saying no to urgent detours and yes to quiet compounding. This isn't passivity, it's precision. Because when you see farther, you act with more care, not less.

The irony, of course, is that long-term clarity often accelerates real impact. When your work is guided by principle rather than panic, it lands more cleanly. When your relationships are chosen for coherence, not convenience, they last longer and support deeper thinking. When your energy is directed with intention instead of reactivity, your decisions multiply instead of dissipating. This is the hidden economy of long-term thinkers. They don't burn out. They compound.

But you can't access that economy if you're tethered to immediacy. And immediacy doesn't just show up in your inbox. It shows up in your mindset. The belief that if you don't post today, you'll disappear. If you don't answer that email, the opportunity will vanish. If you pause to think, someone else will take your place. This is the scarcity script of short-term culture. And it is the death of clear thinking.

Clarity doesn't come from reacting faster. It comes from learning to wait well. From stretching the space between stimulus and response until there is room for vision to speak. From letting things take the time they need, not the time your ego wants. That doesn't mean slowing everything down. It means aligning speed with the signal and moving fast on what matters. Letting go of what doesn't.

So, the question becomes: what does your behavior today signal about your long-term self? Are you living as if you trust the trajectory you're on? Or are you sprinting through your days, hoping speed will compensate for direction? Because clarity is not just about seeing where you are, it's about choosing where you're going with enough presence to shape the path.

And that path, if it's real, will challenge you. You will have to let go of vanity metrics. You will have to resist applause for things that feel misaligned. You will have to confront the parts of your identity that are addicted to urgency. But if you can endure that dissonance, you'll find something rare on the other side. A mind no longer hijacked by the next ping, a schedule distorted by performance, and a life that finally feels like it's aimed at something durable.

That's the gift of long-view clarity. Not certainty. But coherence. A life you can inhabit without pretending. A direction you can trust without constant validation. A mind that no longer needs to outrun the moment, because it knows the moment is part of something larger.

Reflection: Building Your Filter

∞   What's one belief or input you've been absorbing without evaluating lately?
∞   Where in your life do you need more filtration, more boundaries, not more information?
∞   When was the last time you felt mentally spacious? What was absent in that moment?

Filtering isn't rejection. It's choosing what deserves space in your mind.

Part III, Living With Clean Edges

Chapter 17: The Discipline of Discernment

Discernment doesn't shout. It doesn't swagger. It doesn't march into the room with big declarations or clean slogans. It doesn't announce itself as brilliance or wear a badge labeled "clarity." Instead, discernment shows up as hesitation at the right moment, precision in a crowded conversation, or the refusal to chase what everyone else is applauding. It's not the loudest force in the room. It's the most consistent. And in a world obsessed with rapid decisions and instant authority, it is also the most underrated.

Discernment is what remains when reaction fades and insight takes over.

To discern is to distinguish, not just between right and wrong, but between the almost-right and the **actually-right**. Between what looks true and what holds up under pressure. Between what feels good now and what proves helpful later. Between what is yours and what has been offered to you with enough volume that you mistook it for your own.

Clarity without discernment is fragile. It turns into ideology. It calcifies into blind conviction. You might feel confident, even righteous, but you'll be vulnerable to nuance, blind to context, and unfit for complexity. Discernment is what keeps clarity honest. It is the ongoing discipline of checking, refining, observing, not out of self-doubt, but out of respect for the layered nature of reality.

Most people think of discernment as a trait: you have it or you don't. But that's a myth. Discernment is trained. It is forged in the fires of ambiguity, not certainty. And like any discipline, it is not free. It costs time. It costs attention. It costs the comfort of clean answers and the illusion of mastery.

The starting point of discernment is **delayed interpretation**. Not indefinitely, but long enough to let competing signals settle.

Long enough to ask: "What am I being shown? What might I be missing? What's the emotional cost of being wrong here?"

This isn't hesitation for its own sake. It's not indecision masquerading as thoughtfulness. It's the opposite: the refusal to collapse a decision before its accurate dimensions have surfaced.

We live in a world that rewards speed and certainty, which means discernment often goes unrewarded, at least in the short term. People may mistake your pause for weakness. Your careful questioning for cynicism. Your unwillingness to immediately agree due to arrogance or obstruction.

Let them. Your job isn't to match their tempo. Your job is to move in rhythm with reality.

And reality doesn't rush.

Discernment also demands the discipline of **non-attachment to previous versions of yourself**. A clear thinker must be willing to change, not just at the level of opinion, but at the level of *identity*. This is where most people fail. They build brands around their ideas. They anchor their relationships in being "the one who always believes X." They mistake consistency for integrity.

But real discernment is not about staying consistent with your past. It's about staying faithful to what you've most recently discovered to be true.

That requires courage. It requires the willingness to let go of stories that once served you but now distort you. It means revisiting beliefs that made sense in a different context and asking whether they still apply. It means holding your conclusions lightly, even when they feel hard-won.

This doesn't mean you become slippery or unmoored. Quite the opposite. It means your thinking has a spine, not just a surface. A flexible spine. One that bends under new weight and still holds shape.

Discernment is also social. It's the ability to distinguish between feedback that sharpens and feedback that performs. Between those who offer you a challenge rooted in care, and those who package their insecurities as "just being honest." The clear thinker doesn't shut out feedback, but they filter it ruthlessly.

They know that not all criticism is equal. Not all data is neutral. That is not all, advice is insight.

And most importantly, they know the difference between being **perceived as clear** and **being clear**.

That's a key point because much of what passes for discernment today is just rhetorical confidence—the ability to speak in tidy, persuasive soundbites. But discernment often sounds messier than that. It includes phrases like "I don't know yet." Or "I need more time with this." Or "Something about this feels off, even though I can't explain why." That's not ambiguity. That's *honest navigation*.

One of the best markers of a discerning thinker is their comfort with interim conclusions. The ability to move forward with action, even while acknowledging that their map is incomplete. They don't require certainty to proceed. But they refuse to abandon depth to accelerate the timeline.

Discernment is also what helps us avoid another common trap: **moral exhaustion**. In a world saturated with calls to outrage, crises competing for attention, and a culture of ever-expanding causes, the clear thinker must learn to say, "This is not mine to solve. Not now. Not at the expense of what I've chosen to carry."

That's not apathy. It's alignment.

A disciplined mind doesn't collapse under the weight of too many open loops. It closes some, not because they're unworthy, but because the cost of engaging with everything is that you lose the capacity to engage with *anything* deeply.

In that sense, discernment is also an act of mercy. Mercy for your time. Your energy. Your future self.

It's the ability to look at a situation and say, not with judgment, but with clarity, "This doesn't require my opinion," or "This is not mine to pick up."

Because every yes is a no to something else. And clarity is as much about what you *decline to absorb* as what you pursue.

So when you hear the world scream for immediate alignment, instant stances, and definitive positions, pause. Check your signal. Ask yourself what's being asked of you, and whether the urgency is real or merely reflex. Then, choose not from fear or loyalty to an old self, but from **discerned alignment with what matters most now**.

Discernment is slow. It's quiet. It often looks unimpressive. But it's how thinkers outlast noise. It's how they make fewer decisions, and better ones.

It's how they stay clean, even in messy worlds.

Chapter 18: Clarity in Conflict

Clarity is easy in solitude. It sharpens when you're still, when the world is quiet, when no one is challenging your view. Alone, you can hear your thoughts, trace their logic, and feel your values assert themselves. But real life isn't lived in isolation. It's lived in relationships, teams, families, and communities. And it's in those spaces, those charged, dynamic, often combustible spaces, that clarity faces its most significant test, not from confusion, but from **conflict**.

There's a reason most people avoid conflict. It doesn't just risk friction. It risks identity disruption. Conflict threatens the narrative we hold about ourselves: that we are fair, rational, and well-intentioned. It pulls at our edges, exposes our inconsistencies, and drags emotional debris into view. Most of us are not trained for that. We're taught to smooth things over, maintain surface harmony, or launch into righteous defense. But neither avoidance nor aggression produces clarity. They produce loops. Loops that repeat. Loops that accumulate residue.

To be clear, conflict is not about winning. It is not right. It is not to overpower or dissolve tension quickly. It is to **remain intact** in the presence of challenge. To hold coherence under pressure. To stay aware of your reactions, even as they arise. It is to speak with precision in moments when most people grasp for volume. And it is one of the rarest and most vital skills a thinker can cultivate.

Conflict tests your internal filters. Not the ones you apply to information, but the ones that shape your emotional processing. In a heated moment, your nervous system spikes. Your pattern-matching brain lights up, scanning for threat. But the danger is often not the other person; it's what they've triggered. A memory. A hidden insecurity. A belief you've never questioned. Suddenly, you're not in the room anymore. You're somewhere else, reacting to a shadow.

This is where clarity fractures, not because the situation is unclear, but because **you're no longer seeing the problem itself**. You're seeing through the lens of reactivity. And reactivity is almost always reductionist. It collapses complexity into binaries:

right or wrong, safe or unsafe, me or them. The moment you slip into that framework, clarity is lost. You might still argue. You might still dominate. But you're no longer perceiving. You're defending a position, not investigating a truth.

So what does it mean to bring clarity into conflict?

It means remaining inside the actual moment, rather than letting yourself be hijacked by the emotional echoes it activates. That requires awareness. Not just of the external dynamics, who said what, what tone was used, but of your **internal position**. Are you trying to understand, or trying to escape discomfort? Are you listening, or just waiting to respond? Are you holding the other person as a partner in discovery, or casting them as an adversary in your story?

Clarity in conflict is not passive. It doesn't mean suppressing emotion or giving up your stance. It means grounding that stance in truth, not in impulse. It means choosing a language that reflects your real thought, not the performative version you think will gain the upper hand. And it means being willing to be changed, if not in your conclusion, then at least in your understanding of what's being said.

Most conflict escalates not because of disagreement, but because of **misalignment in interpretation**. Two people can be arguing about the same surface issue, responsibility, fairness, timing, while holding entirely different frameworks underneath. One person is protecting autonomy. The other is seeking reassurance. One feels threatened. The other feels abandoned. Without clarity, they never name what's underneath. They keep sparring at the surface. And the real issue remains untouched.

Clarity demands that you investigate those layers. Not to psychoanalyze the other person, but to check your alignment. What's really at stake for you? What are you trying to protect? What does resolution look like: agreement, acknowledgment, or change in behavior? Without that internal map, you wander the terrain of conflict blind. And blind conflict rarely ends well.

To hold clarity in these moments, you must be willing to slow down. Conflict invites speed. It accelerates. Words pile up—emotions snowball. But clarity does not move fast. It requires a different tempo. A breath between sentences. A pause before a rebuttal. A moment of curiosity before the following assumption lands. That slowness isn't weakness. It's control. And it's how you make space for the signal to re-enter the field.

There's a power in saying, in the middle of tension, "I'm not sure what I believe yet," or "Can we pause here?" or "I'm noticing I'm reacting more than I'm thinking." These phrases don't resolve conflict, but they disrupt its velocity. They return the conversation to the ground. And they give both people a chance to recalibrate, not to win, but to see.

Clarity in conflict also means knowing when to step out. Some interactions aren't meant to be resolved. Some people aren't ready to engage with integrity. Some dynamics are too poisoned to clarify without collapse. Walking away, in these moments, isn't failure. It's discernment. It's knowing the difference between a storm worth standing in and a vortex designed to consume you.

But even when you walk away, you can still seek clarity. You can reflect. You can reflect on what was said, what was missed, and the role you played. You can clean the residue. Not to absolve the other person, but to avoid carrying the distortion into your next interaction. Clarity is cumulative. It builds through each moment you choose alignment over ego, perception over performance, curiosity over defense.

Clarity in conflict isn't about avoiding friction, as much as we might wish it were. It's not about sidestepping the discomfort, or engineering conversations so skillfully that no edges ever get touched. Friction, when people care about what they're saying and what they're standing for, is inevitable. The real work, the disciplined, internal work, is learning how to metabolize that friction. To stay with it. To let it sharpen you without slicing through your center. To remain open, even when it stings. Not because pain is noble, but because presence is necessary. Presence is what holds clarity steady when the ground begins to shake.

The ones who can do this, who can stay rooted while the room turns tense, who can hear anger without reacting to it, who can speak truth with weight instead of volume, are not superhuman. They're not morally superior or spiritually enlightened. They've trained. Quietly. Consistently. Often alone. They've spent time building a mind that can hold intensity without turning brittle. A mind that doesn't confuse disagreement with danger. A mind that doesn't retreat just because the emotional temperature has risen.

And this kind of clarity, forged in conflict rather than in calm, earns something subtle but unmistakable: precision under pressure. The ability to say what is true without weaponizing it. To listen deeply without dissolving. To keep the integrity of your thinking intact while remaining in a relationship with another person. That's not just a communication skill. That's a form of power. Not dominance, but sovereignty, the capacity to remain yourself while engaging the full emotional complexity of others.

It takes time to build. And it isn't linear. You'll flinch. You'll get flooded. You'll fall back into old patterns, snap at shadows, and confuse signal with static. But every time you return to the center, every time you catch yourself and reorient, you're reinforcing something real. Not perfection. Not detachment. But the ability to remain clear, even when clarity is hard to come by.

This is what we aim for now. Not the fantasy of conflict-free connection, but the maturity to hold tension without collapse. To stay awake in difficult moments. To let conflict do its deeper work, refining, not eroding; grounding, not exploding. Because clarity in conflict isn't about winning, it's about staying. And the longer you can remain without losing your signal, the more human and the more powerful your clarity becomes.

Chapter 19: Strategic Transparency

Transparency is often misunderstood as a virtue of disclosure. Say everything. Hide nothing. Be radically open. But that kind of transparency, while seductive, is a double-edged sword. Because raw exposure is not the same as clarity, flooding others with unprocessed truth can be just as distorting as withholding it. Overexposure can blur boundaries, confuse intent, and weaken alignment, both internally and in relationships. That's why true transparency must be strategic.

Strategic transparency is not about confession. It's about calibration. It's the decision to reveal truth with timing, with structure, and with **intention**. Not to manipulate, but to serve clarity, yours and theirs. To ensure that what is shared doesn't just unburden the speaker, but sharpens the shared understanding of a moment, a decision, or a relationship.

There is an instinct, especially among those trying to operate with integrity, to err on the side of over-sharing. We imagine that if we say everything we feel, lay out every thought we've had, offer our full context without filter, we'll avoid misunderstanding. But that isn't how communication works. Truth, without coherence, becomes static. And in its raw form, it can confuse more than it clarifies.

We often forget that a signal must be digestible to be truly useful.

So, the work isn't just to be honest. It's to be **constructively honest**.

To get there, we need to untangle transparency from performance. In a culture driven by curated vulnerability and public introspection, the performance of transparency often replaces its substance. People share not to illuminate, but to gain approval. To be seen as deep, brave, or "authentic." But when transparency becomes currency, it loses its grounding in discernment. It becomes a broadcast, not a bond.

Strategic transparency refuses that trap. It begins with a deeper question, not "What do I feel like saying?" but "What would serve clarity here?" That shift changes everything. It moves the focus away from the self as the center of gravity and toward a mutual field of understanding.

This doesn't mean hiding. It means framing. It means asking: what's the clearest version of the truth, right now, for this audience, in this moment? What will open a path forward, not just rehash a path behind?

This is especially important in leadership. Leaders who confuse radical candor with emotional dumping do real damage. Saying "I'm just being honest" is not a free pass for unfiltered projection. People don't need your every worry, every contradiction, every moment of doubt. They need clarity, direction, and, when appropriate, a window into your thinking that helps them feel trusted rather than burdened.

The same applies in close relationships. You don't owe every fear, every insecurity, every mental draft to the people you care about. You owe them integrity. That means truth that's been metabolized, not truth weaponized by impulse. It means choosing what to say, how to say it, and when, based on whether the sharing **builds the bridge or blows it up**.

Transparency, when practiced without structure, becomes emotional outsourcing. We say, "Here, hold this," when what we mean is, "I haven't learned to hold this myself yet." That's not honesty. That's avoidance masquerading as vulnerability.

So how do you practice strategic transparency without becoming opaque or performative?

First, do your reflection. If you haven't sat with your thoughts long enough to find their clean edge, you're not ready to share them. This doesn't mean perfection; it means containment. Clarity requires that you process the fog before exporting it. That you move through your first-draft reactions before putting them on someone else's table.

Second, by naming your intent. Transparency without purpose is just noise. But when you share with an apparent reason, whether it's to align, to repair, or to realign expectations, it creates trust. Not because you said everything, but because what you said was coherent with your role, your values, and your desired outcome.

Third, by recognizing context. What's appropriate in one environment isn't in another. Strategic transparency respects the difference between public and private, between team dynamics and personal growth, between strategic vulnerability and emotional spillage. It honors boundaries, not as avoidance, but as *containers* for insight.

And finally, by remaining aware of timing. The truth told too soon can be as disruptive as a lie. Some truths need space. Some require preparation. Some are best delivered after alignment has been built elsewhere. Strategy doesn't dilute honesty. It makes it more potent.

None of this means playing games. Strategic transparency is not deception. It is not spin. It is not selective omission to preserve power. It is the disciplined act of sharing in the service of clarity, not chaos. It is the work of a mind that respects the impact of words and refuses to treat truth as a blunt object.

This kind of clarity in communication doesn't show up in metrics. It doesn't trend. But it builds something deeper than visibility. It builds trust, not just with others, but with yourself. You begin to trust your timing, your framing, your ability to bring truth without torching the field.

When you learn this discipline, people don't just hear you. They *feel understood* by you. They lean in. Not because you said more than anyone else, but because what you told landed clean. No extra. No pretense. No agenda hidden beneath performative vulnerability.

Just truth, shaped with care.

That is the heart of strategic transparency. Not the floodlight. The focused beam. Not the emotional megaphone, but the well-honed instrument that cuts through distortion without cutting others down.

In a world obsessed with saying more, this kind of thinking becomes rare. But it's not radical. It's practiced. You can learn it. You can teach it. You can build it, slowly, into your code.

Say what's true.

Say what serves.

And say it in a way that keeps your integrity intact, while giving others just enough light to find their way forward.

Chapter 20: The Filtered Mind

There's a point in the pursuit of clarity where you realize the issue isn't that the world is too noisy. It's that your mind is too permeable.

The problem isn't always the volume of inputs, though it often starts there. It's the unfiltered access we grant to those inputs, the porous boundaries we allow between our external environments and our internal narratives. Without filters, even the sharpest mind becomes cluttered. Not because it lacks intelligence, but because it never developed the instinct to separate signal from residue.

Filtering isn't about avoidance. It's not about walling yourself off from ideas, people, or perspectives that challenge you. It's about protecting the sanctity of your thinking from erosion, about conserving mental energy for the decisions that matter. In a world engineered for distraction, a filtered mind isn't just a luxury. It's a necessity for cognitive survival.

And here's the catch: filters are not inherited. They're built.

A filtered mind is shaped slowly, through repeated discernment. It's built by noticing which inputs consistently return a value, and which ones generate emotional noise. It's built by recognizing which conversations restore clarity and which ones leave you second-guessing yourself. It's built by asking, again and again: Is this worth bringing inside?

Because that's the real function of mental filtering, not judgment, not righteousness, but interior stewardship, a filtered mind understands that not everything that demands attention deserves it. Not every opinion is actionable. Not every trend requires a stance. Not every conflict is an invitation to react.

Unfiltered minds react. Filtered minds respond.

The difference is subtle but immense. A reaction is immediate, limbic, and unprocessed. It arises from the need to alleviate discomfort, to address every itch of uncertainty as if it were a fire. But a response is slower. Grounded. It contains choice. It accounts for context. It acknowledges emotion without being ruled by it. And perhaps most importantly, it respects your clarity enough not to auction it off to the loudest bidder.

You don't have to be universally informed to be intelligently engaged. You don't have to follow every headline to be a thoughtful citizen. The most grounded people often appear uninformed, not because they're ignorant, but because they've curated their informational diet with surgical precision. They've learned to trust the downstream signal of deliberate inputs over the upstream chaos of ambient noise.

This isn't detachment. It's mastery.

A filtered mind doesn't avoid responsibility. It assumes more of it. Because once you understand that your mental clarity is the engine behind every high-leverage decision you make, you stop letting other people write code into your system unchecked. You stop giving the benefit of the doubt to sources that erode your discernment. You begin treating your mind like a sovereign domain, open, yes, but not borderless.

Over time, your internal world begins to mirror the cleanliness of your filters. You stop arguing with people who aren't interested in resolution. You stop consuming news that only spikes cortisol. You stop responding to messages that bait you into reactive loops. And not because you've become cold, or aloof, or superior. But because you've chosen clarity over chaos.

You've chosen to think cleanly, even when it's inconvenient.

Especially when it's inconvenient.

There will always be voices that call this selfish. That mistake internalizes discipline for external disengagement. That accuses you of being too controlled, too intentional, too resistant to the whirlwind of shared panic. But those voices rarely understand the cost of clarity. They haven't paid it. They haven't yet experienced what happens when you let the wrong inputs shape your thinking for too long.

When your mental filters degrade, your thoughts become brittle. Your convictions become reactive. Your decisions start to echo the voices you never meant to internalize. Before you know it, your sense of self has been rewritten by ambient noise. Not because you're weak. But because you forgot to install a filter.

So, install one.

Build one.

Reinforce it with everything you learn. Revisit it often. Ask yourself: "What am I letting in right now, and is it mine to carry?" Create rituals that help you pause before absorbing. Teach your nervous system to wait one breath longer before engaging. Surround yourself with people who honor your signal, not just compete for it.

And remember this: a filtered mind is not an empty one. It's not passive. It's precise. It's active in its restraint. It knows that to preserve insight, you must protect your inputs. Not because you're fragile. But because clarity is your edge, and you refuse to let it dull.

Chapter 21: Decision Precision

Most people don't make decisions. They escape them. They delay, hedge, crowdsource, rationalize, and rehearse without committing. They confuse motion with movement and call it prudence. But beneath that hesitation is something more profound: an erosion of precision. Not just in logic, but in self-trust. Not just in analysis, but in *signal recognition*. And without that, even a seemingly thoughtful decision becomes a coin toss with a polished rationale.

To decide precisely is to move not with more information, but with less distortion. It's not about being perfect. It's about *clean contact* with what the moment requires. It's not decisiveness as performance, where action is taken for speed or optics. It's decisiveness as integrity, the ability to commit without collapse, to choose with weight and remain agile.

Precision isn't what happens when all doubt disappears. It's what happens when the doubt is acknowledged, examined, and made irrelevant to the action. The fear doesn't vanish. It just doesn't lead.

Clarity, in this sense, is a precondition for precision. But clarity alone isn't enough. You can see the situation clearly and still struggle to move if your internal decision infrastructure is warped. You might over-value consensus, under-value timing, or use logic to justify what your body has already rejected. Precision isn't just the product of thought. It's the alignment of *thought, emotion, and will*. That's what gives a decision its sharp edge. That's what makes it stick.

We're not trained for that kind of movement. We're trained for analysis. For risk assessments, consider weighted pros and cons, and elaborate on mental models. All of which are useful, until they become *covers*, delaying tactics dressed up as due diligence. Eventually, the clarity you need doesn't live in the data. It lives in the question, "Do I trust myself to live with the consequences of this choice?"

That's the crucible. That's where precision emerges, not in the certainty of the outcome, but in the *clean contact* with the cost of the outcome.

You can't hack that moment. You can only prepare for it.

The preparation doesn't come from running simulations. It comes from practicing decision hygiene. You get better at precision the same way you get better at any discipline: through reps. Small choices, made cleanly. Boundaries set without over-explaining. No's delivered before resentment builds. Yes's chosen before opportunity fades. Each decision is a sharpening of the blade.

And you learn, through repetition, that what makes a decision strong isn't its speed or complexity. It's its *coherence*. The choice reflects who you are now, not who you were a year ago. It honors your current map of the world, not a borrowed model. It doesn't outsource authority. It doesn't smuggle in unresolved fears. It doesn't require a committee to validate it. It lands with a quiet weight, and it holds.

This kind of decision-making doesn't look spectacular from the outside. It's not always fast. It's not always bold. But it's unmistakably *yours*. And when the results come, whether they're wins, losses, or something in between, you can face them fully, because the decision wasn't an accident. It was a stance. Even if it hurt, it was *honest*.

Most noise around decision-making focuses on frameworks. But frameworks without calibration are just scaffolding without a foundation. They make you feel structured. But they don't guarantee contact with the truth. Absolute decision precision begins before the frameworks. It starts in the quiet disciplines: managing your attention, owning your signals, cleaning emotional residue, rejecting false urgency. You can't make clean choices in a dirty environment.

Sometimes precision looks like saying no to something that seems objectively "right" but feels misaligned. Sometimes it looks like choosing speed over safety because you've sensed that delay will cost more than movement. Sometimes it seems like changing your mind, not from insecurity, but because a new truth has earned its way into your field of view.

Precision is dynamic. It flexes. But it never apologizes for its stance. That's what distinguishes it from indecision. Indecision wavers because it's trying to please or protect. Precision moves because it's trying to *serve*.

It also knows the difference between a big decision and a loaded one. Not all stakes are what they appear. Some choices feel heavy because they're entangled with identity, ego, or old trauma. They aren't hard because they're complex. They're hard because they're *charged*. Precision doesn't mean solving that instantly. But it does mean naming it. Saying, "This choice is tangled. I'll clear the charge before I pretend to act clearly."

And then doing that. Walking. Writing. Sitting still, asking more complex questions, and letting your body speak before your brain reasserts control. This is the unglamorous part of clarity. The part that can't be performed, only practiced.

When you train that muscle, you begin to see that decision precision is not just for the big calls. It's how you navigate daily life. It's the tone you choose in a complicated conversation. The shift in priority happens without ceremony. The silence you hold when saying more would only muddy the air.

These are not dramatic acts. But they're decisive. And they accumulate.

Over time, people begin to feel your decisions before you make them. Not because you're predictable, but because your signal is *clean*. You don't waver from fear. You don't stall out of guilt. You don't flinch into complexity because you're afraid to own the moment. You've built a system that keeps you aligned and a rhythm that brings you back when you drift.

Precision doesn't require perfection. But it does require presence.

And that presence, sharpened by clarity, becomes your edge in a world that prefers noise.

Chapter 22: The Long-Term View is the Clear View

Clarity, when compressed into short time frames, tends to mimic panic. It shrinks. It grabs for urgency. It confuses importance with immediacy. But when you stretch your lens, widen the aperture of your thinking beyond the following notification, the following reaction, the next quarter, something remarkable happens. The static fades. The signal sharpens. What felt impossible to parse becomes simple, not because it's easier, but because you're finally seeing it from far enough away.

The long-term view isn't about postponing action. It's about placing action in the correct narrative. It's what allows decisions to breathe, values to settle, and direction to emerge without the distortion of crisis. And in a culture addicted to immediacy, cultivating this kind of perspective is more than a strategy. It's a survival skill.

We're not trained to see long. We're taught to react fast. Metrics are short. Feedback cycles are compressed. Success is tracked in headlines, not legacies. This has consequences, not just in how we operate, but in how we *think*. When you shorten your horizon, you shorten your integrity. You start to optimize for what earns a dopamine hit, not what endures under stress. You mistake cleverness for wisdom. You rush toward a closure that hasn't earned itself.

Clarity doesn't come from speed. It comes from elevation. And nothing elevates faster than asking, "What does this mean in five years? Ten? Who do I become if I keep making decisions this way?" Those questions don't offer immediate relief. But they cut through noise faster than any framework ever could.

The long-term view isn't a retreat from the present. It's a recalibration of what matters. It puts small losses in context. It reveals which tensions are worth enduring. It helps you say no, not because something is bad, but because it doesn't fit the arc of the life you're trying to build. It doesn't match the trajectory of your future clarity.

This isn't an abstraction. It's a strategy. The people who operate with absolute clarity, founders, builders, leaders, thinkers, aren't reacting better. They're thinking longer. They've designed systems, decisions, and relationships that not only survive short-term turbulence but also gain coherence over time. They know the difference between urgency and momentum. And they trust the compounding power of aligned decisions.

But getting there takes practice. It starts with zooming out, not just once, but daily. When a conflict arises, instead of asking, "How do I win this?" ask, "What kind of relationship am I building here?" When a decision feels too complex, ask, "What would I regret not doing if I looked back ten years from now?" These aren't soft questions. They're sharp because they slice through the immediate distortions that make clarity feel so elusive.

Holding the long-term view also protects you from clarity's greatest enemy: performative urgency. There is a need to act quickly to be seen as decisive. The fear of missing out on a moment that probably wasn't yours to begin with. The compulsion to match someone else's pace, even when your tempo is more sustainable. When you abandon the long view, you become vulnerable to movements that were never aligned with your path.

This is especially true in relationships. Without the long view, you optimize for harmony over honesty. You sacrifice integrity for approval. You fear ruptures that might reveal deeper alignment over time. But when you remember the arc, you speak truths that matter more than comfort. You act in ways that future you can be proud of. You lead not for applause, but for resonance.

The long view also reframes failure. What looks like a dead end today may become a turning point tomorrow, but only if you stay in the game long enough to see it. Short-term thinking collapses every setback into an identity crisis. Long-term thinking makes room for adaptation. It says, "Not yet" instead of "Not ever." It lets you lose today without forfeiting the whole.

This mindset isn't about infinite patience. It's about **directional fidelity**. You move forward with clarity, not because you know every step, but because you've aligned yourself with a destination that holds up under scrutiny. And that destination isn't a static goal. It's a state. A way of being. A mind that can move cleanly through complexity because it's no longer hijacked by noise.

Ironically, the long-term view also clarifies what to do right now. When you know what you're building toward, the next step becomes obvious. Not necessarily easy, not always comfortable, but obvious. Because it fits the pattern, it supports the structure. It deepens the root.

Clarity doesn't ask for certainty. It asks for consistency in direction.

And the thinker who holds the long view doesn't just make better decisions. They radiate a different presence. You feel it in their words. In their timing. In their refusal to be rushed. In their ability to walk away without flinching. In their patience when others flail. They are not detached. They are anchored.

This is the edge the world won't teach you. It can't. The world trades in immediacy. It sells speed. It rewards spectacle. And it punishes those who move differently.

But when you build your life around the long view, the fog lifts. Not all at once. Not forever. But long enough to orient yourself again. Long enough to make the next decision not from panic, but from precision.

The long-term view is the clear view. Because it asks not just what works, but what lasts.

And the thinker who holds that view isn't just clearer. They're freer.

Reflection: Designing Thought

- ∞ What personal frameworks or internal rules guide your thinking, consciously or unconsciously?
- ∞ Are any of those structures inherited, outdated, or no longer serving your clarity?
- ∞ Where could you use more structure, not more content?

Clarity doesn't mean thinking less. It means thinking in ways that hold truth without breaking under it.

Part IV, Practicing Clarity in the Real World

Chapter 23: Clarity in Conversation

Clarity is often imagined as a solitary achievement, something you arrive at in silence, with enough time and distance to think clearly. But the moment you open your mouth and step into conversation, that clarity is tested. Not because others are malicious or irrational, but because dialogue is a collision of frames. And in that collision, precision gets warped, emotion leaks in, and ambiguity spreads.

Conversations are where clarity either hardens or dissolves. They are where your internal filters meet someone else's lived experience. Where your frameworks intersect with competing truths. And if you're not careful, the very language you use to express insight becomes the vector for its distortion.

This is why clarity in conversation is not about being articulate. It's about being **anchored**. When you're anchored, you don't speak to fill the silence or to win approval. You talk because you've taken the time to think. And you know what matters enough to say. But that alone isn't enough. Because even if your thoughts are clean, your delivery can still distort them.

Clarity in conversation begins before the first word. It starts with intention. Are you trying to connect, to correct, to control, to be understood, or to understand? Most conversational fog comes not from poor vocabulary but from **unexamined motive**. You can hear it when someone is explaining, but asking for permission. Or arguing, but asking to be heard, and/or nodding along while mentally disengaged. These mismatches pollute the space. The signal degrades because the intent isn't honest.

True clarity requires *conversational alignment*: that your words, tone, and presence match your purpose.

But here's the catch: most people don't want clarity in conversation. They want a resolution. Agreement. Peace. Or power. Clarity, on the other hand, is messier. It sometimes leads to friction. Because to be clear is to risk being different. To be clear is to say, "This is what I see," even when it doesn't match the consensus, especially when it doesn't.

This is why clarity demands courage. Not loudness. Not dominance. But the willingness to *let go of being liked in exchange for being understood.* It's a difficult trade, particularly in emotionally charged dialogue. And it's one many people avoid. They'll dilute what they believe to preserve comfort. They'll hedge truth into vagueness. They'll perform an agreement. And slowly, their ability to speak erodes.

But clarity doesn't require you to dominate the room. It requires you to **hold your shape** in it. To bring the full weight of your thought to the table without demanding that others collapse into it.

That's where clarity differs from conviction. Conviction says, "I'm right." Clarity says, "Here's what I see." The former shuts down the conversation. The latter opens a window, inviting others to respond with their view. And when two people speak from clarity, rather than from defense, something rare happens: **mutual refinement**. Not an argument. Not surrender. But the sharpening of thought through exposure to difference.

That doesn't happen automatically. It requires something most conversations skip: **reflective precision**. The willingness to say, "Here's what I think I heard. Is that accurate?" Or "When you said that, I felt X. Was that your intent?" These clarifying moves aren't indulgent; they're essential because interpretation is distortion's playground. Every phrase you say is run through someone else's filters, cognitive, emotional, cultural, and historical. And what they hear is rarely exactly what you meant unless you check. Unless you ask. Unless you slow the loop down enough to match the signals.

People often resist this level of precision because it feels awkward. It breaks the rhythm. But that rhythm is usually noise masquerading as flow. Its momentum is built on an assumption. And the longer it runs, the more off-course you both get. Clarity means pausing, even mid-conversation, to verify alignment before building on a misunderstanding.

But what happens when the other person doesn't want clarity? What if they wish to dominate, or comfort, or vent?

Then your clarity becomes a boundary. You don't force clean thought on someone unwilling to receive it. But you also don't surrender yours to keep the peace. You state your intention. You listen deeply. And if the exchange becomes manipulative or incoherent, you withdraw, not from the person, but from the performance. You refuse to co-author confusion.

This is especially hard in close relationships. Because clarity often reveals uncomfortable truths: mismatched values, unsaid resentments, diverging trajectories. And we're taught to preserve harmony at all costs. But false harmony isn't peace, it's delay. Delay of reckoning. Delay of honesty. Delay of growth. And when you avoid hard clarity to stay liked, you end up erasing yourself.

Clean conversation, by contrast, is not sterile. It's not robotic. It's alive. It has edges. It breathes. It adjusts without abandoning. It holds shape without aggression. And it treats the other person not as an opponent or audience, but as a **thinking partner**. That's what makes it rare. That's what makes it powerful.

If you want to develop clarity in conversation, you don't start by rehearsing what to say. You start by listening to yourself. How do you speak when you're afraid? When you're trying to prove something? When you want to disappear? When you're hoping they'll rescue your thought because you don't trust it yet?

This is where clarity is won or lost. In the *posture* of your presence. Not just the words you use, but the shape you take when using them.

Do you lean in or back away? Do you escalate or inquire? Do you collapse at the first sign of disagreement, or do you root more deeply in your intent?

These are not rhetorical questions. They are diagnostic tools for your inner clarity. Because in conversation, your thinking gets revealed, not just in argument, but in your *ability to remain clear while being seen.*

That is the highest level of conversational clarity. Not performance, not persuasion, but presence. Saying only what you mean. Hearing beyond what was said. Refusing to fill the silence with noise. And allowing the truth, whatever shape it takes, to come into the room without flinching.

That's clarity in conversation. Not louder. Cleaner.

Chapter 24: Cognitive Minimalism

There is a hidden cost to every bit of information you consume. Every notification, every headline, every passing opinion that enters your mental field draws on the same finite pool of cognitive resources. And the irony is, we collect these fragments in the name of being "informed," as if more input means more wisdom. But the opposite is often true. The more mental clutter we carry, the more our attention splinters. The more we chase relevance, the less we remember what clarity feels like.

That's why clean thinking, in practice, demands **cognitive minimalism**, a conscious, daily subtraction of what doesn't serve clarity.

This is not about tuning out the world or pretending ignorance is virtue. It's about something more radical: **curating your attention like it's your most precious asset**, because it is. It's the foundation of every insight, every decision, every moment of presence. And yet we waste it, leaving the gates of our minds open to every passing distraction like a home with no doors.

Cognitive minimalism begins with a basic recognition: **not all information is created equal**. Some sharpen. Some blurs. Some add weight. Some adds noise. If you don't distinguish between them, your brain defaults to stimulation, not substance. And stimulation, over time, feels like momentum. But it's not. It's the illusion of relevance without the architecture of understanding.

A minimalist mind isn't an empty one. It's a mind that's **deliberately pruned**, like a bonsai, not because it rejects complexity, but because it knows that **clarity can't survive in overgrowth**.

The hardest part of adopting cognitive minimalism is not the absence of input. It's the discomfort of silence. The first time you step back from the flood, the scroll, the inbox, the news, the dopamine loop, you're left with something unfamiliar: yourself. And for many people, that self has been neglected. Numbed. Outpaced by the rhythm of digital life. Minimalism brings it back to the forefront. And not everyone is ready for the reintroduction.

But that discomfort is part of the process. You begin to notice which thoughts are yours and which are residues of someone else's urgency. You start to feel the difference between curiosity and compulsion. You remember what it's like to follow a line of thinking to the bottom, instead of abandoning it the moment it gets complicated or tedious. That's the power of subtraction. It clears space, not just for better thoughts, but for **longer ones**.

In a culture obsessed with optimization, minimalism can feel like regression. Like doing less. But it's the opposite. It's doing **what matters**, with less interference. It's creating the mental equivalent of deep work conditions: no clutter, no noise, just you and the problem, or the question, or the pattern. You get to know the architecture of your perception, how you move through ambiguity, how you handle contradiction, how you hold tension without rushing to resolve it. That's clarity. But you don't get there by consuming more. You get there by consuming wisely.

Minimalism is not just about what you avoid. It's about what you **invite in more fully**. A single book read with full attention is worth more than a thousand tweets skimmed. A quiet moment of reflective writing can produce more insight than a month of reacting to news. It's not that depth is superior by default. It's that depth that gives you space to recognize what's real, and time to choose how you'll respond to it.

This is where minimalist clarity becomes a design principle. You begin to build systems around it. Not rigid routines, but **guardrails for attention**. You check the news once a day, not once an hour. You silence non-essential notifications. You curate your inputs the way a sommelier curates wine, based on nuance, not noise. You stop performing responsiveness as a badge of relevance. And in its place, you cultivate **presence**.

Presence is the fruit of minimalism. Not presence as performative mindfulness, but as **undivided participation** in what you're doing, who you're with, and what you're thinking. It's the experience of being entirely located in your mind again. Not borrowed, not hijacked, but returned.

This return isn't passive. It's defended. Every day, the world will try to reclaim your mind through urgency, outrage, novelty, and shame. But a minimalist thinker doesn't flinch at the pressure. They know how to say no without guilt. They know how to disconnect without apology. Because they've learned that the cost of constant connection is not just time, it's identity. You become what you react to. And if you respond to everything, you become **unrecognizable to yourself**.

That's the hidden danger of modern cognition. Not just burnout, but **self-erasure**. The erosion of the clean line between stimulus and self. Minimalism restores that line. It says: I will not carry every signal. I will not chase every alert. I will not confuse busyness with discernment. I will subtract what isn't a signal, so I can *hear* what is.

The clarity that comes from this is not euphoric. It's grounded. Unremarkable in the best way. Like a room with nothing out of place. Like a page without error. Like a conversation without an agenda. You don't even realize how much noise you were carrying until it's gone. And then you look at your mind and see, finally, a space worth trusting again.

That's cognitive minimalism. Not silence for its own sake, but **space made sacred** by the clarity it protects.

Chapter 25: When Clarity Costs You

Everyone loves clarity until it asks for something in return. Until it requires the courage to say what you see, even when it threatens your comfort. Until it pulls you out of the crowd, interrupts the flow, or makes you unrecognizable to the very people you once aligned with. That's the part no one warns you about. That clarity isn't always rewarded. Sometimes, it costs you.

The fantasy is that once you learn to think clearly, the world will welcome your insight. That your refined perception will lead to better outcomes, stronger relationships, and deeper trust. And sometimes, it does. But often, especially at first, it isolates. Because clarity breaks illusions. And illusions are the glue in many social arrangements, teams, partnerships, friendships, and even families.

When you start to see clearly, you also begin to see differently. You notice what others overlook. You question what others accept. You hesitate where others rush in. And that makes people uncomfortable. Not because you're trying to cause discomfort, but because your very presence disrupts a rhythm they've learned to dance to.

This is the first cost of clarity: **alienation**. The quiet distance that opens when you stop nodding along to things that no longer make sense. The moments where you speak with care and accuracy, only to be told you're "overthinking," "too serious," or "difficult." These phrases aren't about you. They're defense mechanisms. Signals that someone would rather preserve the mood than examine the meaning.

And this is where many people retreat. Not because they lack clarity, but because they can't bear the social friction it brings. So they water themselves down. They soften what they see. They perform an agreement they no longer feel. And over time, their thinking becomes foggy again, not because they forgot how to see, but because they chose not to.

Clarity, when it's honest, is not always pleasant. It reveals dependencies. It names trade-offs. It calls out your complicity. It shows you where you've been sleepwalking. And then it asks: Will you act on this? Or will you pretend you didn't notice?

That question is what gives clarity its cost. Because seeing clearly and not acting is painful. But to act often requires **letting go of things you once relied on**, such as roles, routines, and relationships. You may find yourself outgrowing environments that once felt like home. Not because you're better than them, but because you're no longer blurred enough to blend in.

The world runs, in large part, on managed ambiguity. On the polite fiction that everything is fine. On the unspoken agreement that we won't name what's obvious if doing so risks the group's comfort. Clarity breaks that pact. It doesn't do it cruelly, but it does it honestly. And honesty, even when soft, can feel like violence in an environment built on subtle denial.

So what do you do when your clarity costs you? When it leaves you standing alone, or misunderstood, or labeled?

You ground yourself in the reason you sought it in the first place.

You remember that clarity wasn't a vanity project. It was a return to self-trust. It was a reclamation of your inner signal. It was a way to navigate life without outsourcing your perception to consensus or trend.

And then you rebuild. Not with noise. Not with force. But with people and places that reward coherence over conformity. With systems that support presence over performance. With relationships that welcome discomfort as a pathway to depth. They exist. But you can't find them while pretending. You find them when you show up, even when it costs you approval.

There's another cost, too, one people rarely admit: **grief**. The grief of realizing how much of your life was shaped by what you didn't see. The missed opportunities. The false investments. The years spent defending positions you no longer believe in. Clarity brings that flood. Not to punish you, but to unburden you. To let you feel the weight you carried while pretending not to notice the drift.

You can't outrun that grief. But you can metabolize it. You can use it as evidence, not of failure, but of growth. Because to see, finally, after years in the fog, is a kind of rebirth. And birth is always messy. It always requires leaving something behind.

There's also the cost of **an urgent withdrawal**. Clarity slows you down. It makes you pause where others push. It prompts questions that complicate the plan. And in a culture addicted to speed, that pause can make you feel broken. Why aren't you moving? Why aren't you excited? Why do you keep challenging things that "work"?

But the truth is, most things that "work" are just optimized illusions. They get results, sure, but at the cost of depth, integrity, and long-term viability. Clarity lets you see that. And once you see it, you can't unsee it. You may try to go back. To rejoin the hustle. To silence the quiet voice that says, "This isn't aligned." But it won't work because you'll know what it costs you to be clear. And that knowledge won't let you betray yourself so easily again.

The final cost worth mentioning is perhaps the subtlest: **peace with uncertainty**. Clarity doesn't promise certainty. It promises precision about what's known and what isn't. And that means you'll live with open loops. With the tension of the unsolved. With the humility of not always having the answer. That humility can look like weakness to those who mistake confidence for competence. But it's not. Its strength. Quiet, disciplined strength. The kind that doesn't need to know how to perform. The kind that makes room for discovery.

You won't always be thanked for this. You won't always be liked for it. But you will sleep with a lighter conscience. You will think with less distortion. And you will act with more integrity.

That is what clarity gives you. And that is what it costs.

Chapter 26: Clean Thinking Under Pressure

It's easy to think clearly when life gives you space. When you've had time to rest, when emotions are settled, when decisions aren't on fire. But absolute clarity, the kind that matters most, doesn't show up in calm. It reveals itself in **pressure**. In the moment when everything tightens and time compresses and everyone's looking to you for certainty you may not yet have.

Most people crack under that weight. Not because they're weak, but because they never trained for it. They treated clarity as a luxury. A slow ritual reserved for quiet Sunday mornings or abstract thought experiments. They didn't build it for war. They didn't test it in chaos. And so when pressure arrived, they reached for instinct, not insight. They reacted, not responded. And in doing so, they lost what little clarity they had.

Clean thinking under pressure is a skill. And like any skill, it's earned. It's not given to the smartest or most seasoned. It belongs to the person who's willing to do the one thing pressure punishes: **slow down**.

That's the first principle. In high-pressure moments, your body speeds up. Your nervous system prepares for battle. Your perception narrows. Your voice tightens. Your awareness shrinks. And everything in you screams: decide now. Move now. Say something now.

But clarity doesn't live in panic. It lives in **the present**. And presence only returns when you reclaim your pace.

This doesn't mean you stall. It means you *assert agency over tempo*. You take one deep breath. You ask one good question. You pause for one beat longer than comfort allows. In that moment, you're doing more than buying time. You're resetting your signal. You're telling your mind: I'm in control of the frame, not the frame of me.

But pace alone isn't enough. Clean thinking under pressure also requires **preparation without rigidity**. That is, you have frameworks. You've built clarity into your worldview. You've rehearsed your mental models. But you're not married to them. Because pressure brings novelty. And if your models can't bend, they break. The clear thinker doesn't cling to prior certainty. They adapt with intent. They hold principles, not scripts.

This is what separates clean thought from clever thought. Cleverness works until the environment shifts. Clarity endures because it knows what matters and can reshape around it. It's flexible, not frantic.

You'll recognize clean thinking under pressure by its **disciplined humility**. The person isn't loud. They're focused. They ask precise questions. They seek ground truth before making declarations. They resist the allure of easy answers. And they don't pretend to know more than they do.

This isn't paralysis. It's pace-matched cognition. And it's rare. Because most people, when confronted by intensity, collapse into performance. They say what they think others want to hear. They act for approval, not accuracy. They chase outcomes at the cost of orientation. And in doing so, they manufacture fog.

But the disciplined thinker does the opposite. They focus not just on the decision, but on the *conditions under which they're deciding*. They ask: What do I know? What do I assume? What's changing? What signal matters now? And they act only when that scan is complete.

This doesn't mean they move slowly. It means they move **consciously** with just enough friction to keep their thinking honest.

There's a phrase in aviation: "aviate, navigate, communicate." First, fly the plane. Then figure out where you are. Then talk to others. It's a hierarchy of clarity under stress. And it maps cleanly onto mental pressure. First, stabilize yourself. Then assess reality. Then express your thinking. Most people reverse this. They talk first, often before flying the plane in their mind. And that's how confusion spreads.

Clean thinkers don't just manage their signal. They prevent signal collapse in the room. They protect the cognitive environment. They limit noise. They name tensions. They avoid blame. And in doing so, they **become clarity multipliers**, even in chaos.

That's a challenging role. It can feel thankless. It often means being the calm one when others are spiraling. The grounded one when tempers flare. But it's not stoicism for its own sake. It's a tactical choice. Because they know panic makes poor patterns. And drama makes dumb decisions.

Still, clarity under pressure isn't about being emotionless. It's about **not being owned by the emotion**. It's noticing the internal spike and choosing not to outsource it. It's allowing the fear, anger, or doubt to surface, without giving it the mic. That requires self-awareness. And it requires practice. You don't develop that skill in the middle of the fire. You build it through **daily friction**. Through small moments where you pause instead of reacting. Where you verify instead of assuming. Where you wait one more breath before speaking.

Over time, those micro-skills compound. And one day, in a real moment of pressure, you'll feel it. The world will start to spin. People will look to you. And you'll do something different. You'll slow your breathing. You'll check the facts. You'll hold your tone. You'll resist the spin. And you'll think clearly, not because the situation allows it, but because *you trained for it*.

That's the quiet reward. Not perfection. Not unshakable poise. But the ability to access your clarity when it matters most. When the cost of confusion is high. When the margin for error is thin. When the people around you are stuck in reaction.

You don't need to be fearless. You need to be **signal-aware**. You need to protect the architecture of thought under pressure. You need to know how to stay present inside the storm without becoming part of it.

That's clean thinking under pressure.

Chapter 27: Living Your Clarity

You can study clarity. You can practice it. You can even write about it with precision and passion. But until you live it, until it becomes the way you move through the world, it remains theoretical. A preference, not a principle. A lens, not a lifestyle.

Living your clarity is not a declaration. It's not something you announce or wear like a badge. It's quieter than that. More inconvenient. More demanding. It's what shows up in the small, private choices. The ones no one sees. The ones that reveal whether your thoughts are truly clean or just cleverly disguised.

It begins with **alignment**. Not the grand, sweeping kind. The daily kind. The email you don't send because it muddies the waters. The meeting you decline because it exists only to preserve ambiguity. The friend you gently distance yourself from, not out of anger, but because the dynamic no longer supports mutual honesty. These are not dramatic acts. They are *clarifying* acts. You choose coherence over comfort—integrity over inertia.

But living your clarity also means **taking the hits**. Because sometimes, clarity offends. Not because you're being unkind, but because you're being **unmistakable**. You're no longer hedging your speech to manage others' reactions. You're no longer pretending not to notice what's broken. And that refusal to dilute makes people flinch, especially in cultures built on politeness, productivity, or performative positivity.

You will be misunderstood. You will be told you're rigid, or intense, or "too much." And in those moments, you'll be tempted to dim again. To round your edges. To trade truth for harmony. But clarity lived is clarity **protected**. You don't abandon it to be more palatable. You learn to hold it with grace. To speak cleanly without contempt. To have boundaries without defensiveness. To remain open, without becoming porous.

That balance takes time. Early on, living clearly can feel isolating. You'll notice how much of life runs on scripts. How many conversations are rituals of evasion? How many workplaces reward noise over signal? It can make you cynical. But if you stay with it, if you move past that disillusionment, something else appears: **depth**.

Your relationships change, not by accident, but by filtration. You attract people who want signal, not spin—those who welcome hard truths and name their own. You start building systems, teams, partnerships, and routines that run on clarity instead of coercion. And suddenly, you don't need to manage perception as much. Because the people around you *expect honesty*, and are honest in return.

That is the unseen dividend of clarity lived: you spend less energy **pretending**. You stop performing optimism. You stop faking certainty. You stop carrying the weight of everyone else's expectations. And you begin to operate from a deeper center, not reactive, not anxious, not performative. Just real.

It sounds simple. But it isn't. Because the world rewards projection. It rewards smoothness over sharpness. It rewards knowing the right thing to say, not the truest. To live is to **opt out of that game**, not with bitterness, but with precision.

You don't become unkind. You become *undefended*. You stop spinning. You say what you see. You ask questions that cut through. And when you don't know, you say so, without shame.

This has consequences. It will cost you things you once valued. But it gives you something rarer: a kind of **internal ease** that's impossible to fake. Not because everything is sure, but because *you* are no longer at war with your perception. You trust what you see. You've done the work. You've verified your filters. And so when things are murky, you can wait. When things are pressured, you can pause. And when things are clear, you can act, cleanly, precisely, without drama.

Living your clarity also changes how you relate to power. You stop seeking it through consensus. You stop treating approval as validation. You start asking: Does this system support clarity? Does this conversation sharpen or blur? Does this decision align with how I want to think and live?

You become harder to manipulate. Not harder to influence, just harder to distort. Because you're signal-led, you notice noise early. You don't chase excitement unless it's grounded. You don't let urgency seduce you. You stay with things longer. You discard things faster. And through it all, you protect what matters: *the architecture of your attention*.

That is what clarity becomes, not just a thought practice, but a life practice. One that shows up in your calendar. In your tone. In your inbox. In how you name your own needs. In how you let others go. In how you stay present when others flee.

It's not glamorous. Most of the time, it's unremarkable. But there's a sharpness to it. A hum beneath the surface. You feel it when you're living clearly: that sense of being clean on the inside. No residue. No internal edits. Just you, as you are, showing up for what's real.

And maybe that's the deepest reason to live this way. Not to be admired. Not to be efficient. But to be **intact**. To move through the world without fracturing your perception at every turn. To get to the end of the day and know, quietly, that you didn't betray your sensemaking. That you held the thread. That you spoke when it mattered. That you remained clean, even when the world begged you not to be.

That's the quiet integrity of a life lived in clarity.

Not flashy. Not perfect. But *true*.

Reflection: Listening Inward

- ∞ How do you usually respond to feedback, external or internal?
- ∞ When does your inner critic sound like a signal? When does it sound like noise?
- ∞ What feedback loop in your life needs redesigning, not just reacting?

Clarity isn't passive observation. It's a conscious relationship to your signals.

Part V, The Clarity Continuum

Chapter 28: Regression to the Fog

Clarity, once gained, is never guaranteed. It doesn't install like software. It doesn't lock in like a belief. It lives, or dies, in motion. It decays in silence, in comfort, in the unnoticed slide back into old environments, old behaviors, and old mental habits. And that decay has a name: **regression to the fog**.

You can be thinking clearly on Monday and spinning by Thursday. Not because you forgot everything you learned, but because life got loud. Because stress hit. Because you skipped your habits. Because someone else's chaos became yours. Clarity is perishable. It fades when you stop maintaining it, and most people don't notice the slip until they've fully returned to the fog.

The tragedy of regression isn't the fog itself. It's the fact that you no longer fit inside it. Once you've seen the signal, noise is harder to live with. Once you've experienced the peace of clean perception, distortion feels like sand in your brain. But that doesn't mean you won't return to it. You will. Everyone does. The question is, *how fast do you catch it*?

Regression is usually subtle. It doesn't announce itself with failure. It arrives wrapped in routine. You stop asking good questions. You skim instead of reading. You react instead of reflecting. You seek stimulation instead of a signal. You begin confusing motion for momentum. And slowly, your inner compass starts spinning again.

Sometimes it starts with **external overexposure**, too much media, too many opinions, too many conversations without edges. Your attention gets diluted. You start checking your phone more, but reading less. You scroll but don't absorb. You listen, but you don't hear. You stop seeing the world cleanly, and instead, you start *feeling* it in fragments, agitated, distracted, slightly ashamed that you can't quite articulate why.

Other times, the regression comes from **internal erosion**. You compromise a little, ignoring a truth you once named. You avoid a conversation that needs clarity. You stay in a place you've outgrown. Not because you're malicious, but because you're tired. Because the clarity muscle felt heavy that day. And so you borrow ease instead of holding your edge.

And that's the danger: the fog is cozy. It's familiar. It lets you off the hook. It tells you that nuance is exhausting, and certainty is safer, even if it's false. It whispers that maybe clarity was just a phase. That may be fog is normal. That maybe questioning everything was overthinking.

But then, one morning, you wake up and realize you've lost signal. You don't trust your instincts. You hesitate to speak. You rely on external validation. And worst of all, you don't feel like *yourself*. The version of you that could pause and see and name, that person's gone quiet.

That's the moment that matters. The moment you **notice** the slide. That moment is your invitation back. Not through force. Not through shame. But through **returning**.

You don't claw your way back to clarity with a single act. You **rebuild**. You return to the rituals that made you precise. You start scanning your inputs. You sit in silence again, not for peace, but for reconnection. You write. You ask yourself what you're pretending not to know. You say no. You clear the calendar. You breathe.

And slowly, the fog begins to lift, not all at once. But with every re-engaged signal, every choice to notice instead of numb, you remember this is how I think when I'm clear. This is what I see when I'm not spinning. This is who I am when I'm not hijacked by noise.

No version of clarity is immune to regression. The goal isn't perfection. It's recovery speed. It's awareness. It's noticing earlier each time. It's building such a deep familiarity with your internal clarity that the moment something feels off, you don't gaslight yourself, you *investigate*.

Regression becomes your **teacher**. It shows you where your systems failed. It shows you which people corrode your perception. It shows you how fragile your attention is. And that knowledge makes you humble. But it also makes you stronger. Because now, clarity is no longer a mood. It's a method—a practiced return.

One of the greatest misconceptions is that regression is a weakness. The need to recalibrate means you failed. It doesn't. It means you're human. It means your mind is dynamic. It means you've evolved enough to notice the drift.

And drift is inevitable. But drifting doesn't mean drowning. It means it's time to re-anchor. To check the tools. To verify the map. And to choose, deliberately, to move back into alignment.

That's what it means to live with clarity as a practice. You don't assume it. You don't defend it. You **cultivate it**, over and over again. And when the fog returns, you don't panic. You say: I've been here before. And I know the way back.

That's not failure. That's fluency.

Chapter 29: Signal Integrity

Clarity is not just about how you think. It's about how you **transmit**. It's one thing to reach clean conclusions inside your head; it's another thing entirely to communicate those conclusions to the world without distortion, erosion, or noise. And this is where many would-be clear thinkers stumble: not in their cognition, but in their **expression**.

If your signal is muddy, your intentions don't matter. If your clarity doesn't survive the translation from thought to word, it may as well not exist. The gap between clean thinking and clean transmission is where reputations fracture, teams unravel, trust dissolves, and decisions collapse.

So the question becomes: once you've achieved clarity, how do you **preserve its integrity**?

Signal integrity begins with **linguistic precision**. Most people speak in approximations. They use vague qualifiers, ambiguous metaphors, emotionally charged phrasing, or worse, borrowed language that sounds smart but signals nothing. Clarity requires a different ethic. You choose the *clearest, most accurate word*, not the most persuasive or popular one. You trim filler. You disarm defensiveness. You resist jargon unless your audience breathes it.

But precision alone doesn't make signal land. You also need **audience awareness**. Clean thinkers adapt their expression without corrupting their core message. They translate without diluting. They don't condescend, but they also don't expect others to share their exact lens. Signal integrity means clarity **for the other person**, not just for yourself.

This is not about being clever. It's about *transparency of intent*. Are you speaking to illuminate, or to impress? Are you clarifying, or posturing? Clean signal doesn't seek credit. It seeks coherence.

That becomes especially crucial when clarity carries a cost. When your clean conclusion upsets someone, or contradicts the consensus, or surfaces an uncomfortable truth. In those moments, the temptation is to soften, hedge, or delay. And sometimes, a little friction buffering helps. But too often, the fear of conflict becomes a fog machine. You lose your message in a cloud of qualifiers and social performance. And what could have been a clean line of insight becomes an interpretive mess.

Signal integrity is the courage to say the thing, without venom, without apology, without distortion. Not recklessly. Not rudely. But unmistakably.

That doesn't mean you say everything. Clarity isn't verbal vomit. It's **intentional framing**. You ask yourself: what truth here is most essential? What context do I need to honor? What will sharpen the room instead of flattening it?

Clean expression often means saying *less*. Not because you're withholding, but because you've edited your thinking so well that the message doesn't need dressing. You've stripped the noise. You've anchored in relevance. You've removed the cognitive static that forces listeners to decode your real intent.

And then comes the final, and most misunderstood, dimension of signal integrity: **tone**.

A clean signal doesn't land if your tone sabotages it. This isn't about being nice. It's about being *undistracting*. If your voice is laced with resentment, panic, superiority, or shame, your words will be filtered through that noise. And instead of hearing the signal, people will react to your emotional static. This is where many brilliant thinkers fail; they say the right thing in the wrong emotional envelope and wonder why it backfires.

To preserve tone, you need **emotional hygiene**. You don't speak mid-flinch. You don't send emails while spinning. You pause. You clarify your intent. You ask yourself: What am I trying to protect? What's the cleanest way to express this truth *without burdening the other person with my mess*?

That level of discipline doesn't come naturally. Especially in environments that reward speed, outrage, or hot takes. But if you care about signal, *genuinely care*, you learn to delay expression until it's clean enough to carry the weight of your clarity.

Over time, something interesting happens. People start to associate you with coherence. With sharp, calm, honest thinking. You become someone they listen to, not because you speak often, but because when you do, you don't waste their cognitive bandwidth. You don't make them guess. You don't flood them with abstraction. You give them a signal.

That kind of presence is rare. And powerful. Not because it dominates, but because it **builds trust**. In an era of noise, a clean signal is *magnetic*. It gives people relief. It lets them lower their guard. It shows them that truth and clarity can co-exist with care.

And so signal integrity isn't just an intellectual virtue. It's a social contract. It's how you navigate life without confusion. It's about building cultures that don't waste time. It's how you become a leader people trust, not because you're always right, but because you don't spin. You don't distort. You don't hide.

You say what needs to be said, cleanly, calmly, and without fog.

That's the ethic of the clear communicator. Not just to think cleanly, but to **signal cleanly**, when it counts.

Chapter 30: Social Clarity

You may find clarity alone, but you prove it among people.

It's one thing to sit in stillness, journaling with precision, mentally sorting signal from noise in a quiet room. It's another to carry that clarity into the swirl of relationships, where people project, defend, evade, and mirror. Social interaction, by its nature, introduces distortion. Everyone brings their frame, their fog, their unfinished thought patterns. And if you're not careful, their noise becomes your noise.

That's why social clarity isn't just a bonus feature of clean thinking. It's an advanced test. It shows whether your clarity has edges. Whether it holds under pressure. Whether it survives *other people's confusion* without retreating or retaliating.

Most of us aren't taught to maintain personal boundaries in social settings. We're taught to be agreeable, diplomatic, or palatable. We learn to smooth the signal in favor of harmony, or weaponize it in favor of dominance. We mask truth with performance. We make people comfortable at the cost of coherence. Or we mistake aggression for honesty and call it "being real" when in fact it's just unprocessed emotion masquerading as clarity.

Actual social clarity lives somewhere else, between collapse and control. It's not about being blunt. It's about being unmistakable **without triggering unnecessary defense**. You say what is true *without abandoning care*. You give people a signal, but not a spike. You name what's present, but not to punish.

This requires two things: internal grounding and external generosity.

Internal grounding means your clarity is anchored in *self-regulation*. You don't enter conversations to win. You don't escalate to prove. You don't defer to avoid. You don't hijack others to discharge your discomfort. You know what you see. You've verified your perception. And you don't need others to agree with you to stay centered in it.

This makes you dangerous in the best way. Not volatile, *stable*. Not unfeeling, *unhooked*. You don't need people's approval to maintain your internal clarity. That means you can listen. You can be changed. You can be moved by truth without losing your signal.

But grounding isn't enough. Clarity becomes powerful only when combined with **generosity**. That means honoring the limits of other people's readiness. It means recognizing that even when your message is clear, it may still get lost in someone else's static. It means knowing when to speak and when to wait. When to press, and when to pause.

Generosity does not mean enabling confusion. It means **distributing the signal in a way that allows people to receive it**. Sometimes that looks like asking questions instead of making declarations. Sometimes it means framing your truth with context, not to justify but to locate. Sometimes it means walking away, not because you're afraid, but because clarity can't be forced into a closed mind.

Social clarity also means being okay with not being liked. If your clarity always wins you applause, you're probably not being clear. You're being *convenient*. An accurate signal disrupts stale agreements. It surfaces unspoken assumptions. It confronts collective denial. And when it does, people react. They project. They push back. They accuse.

That's part of the deal. The cost of clarity in the community is **being misunderstood**. But the gift is that, over time, the right people stay. The ones who crave reality. Those who value honest frames. Who can tell when you're speaking from ego or essence? Who helps you see when your clarity is slipping?

Because social clarity isn't a solo project, it requires mirrors. It's sustained in ecosystems where the signal is valued, not punished, where questions are welcomed, not resented, where people are more loyal to the truth than to the hierarchy.

If you find yourself in spaces where clarity is consistently penalized, where speaking cleanly earns you exclusion, or silence is the only safe path, pay attention. That's not your failure. That's *fog enforced by structure*. And clarity cannot survive long in systems built on distortion. Sometimes, the clearest move is to **exit**.

But more often, the opportunity is subtler. It's in the everyday moments where you choose to keep your distance from *people*. When someone makes a vague accusation, you don't match their vagueness. You ask for specificity. When conflict emerges, you don't triangulate. You go directly. When expectations are unclear, you name them. When tension rises, you name the frame. You make the implicit explicit. You give things shape.

That doesn't always make things easier. Clarity often increases friction. But it's *honest friction*. Productive friction. It burns off fog. It creates the conditions for alignment. And it liberates people from the games that keep them stuck.

As you begin to live with more internal clarity, something inevitable unfolds: your relationships start to shift. Not because you force them to, but because the terms of connection subtly realign. You no longer find it bearable to linger in spaces built on performance. The conversations that once passed for intimacy, full of surface-level gestures, masked discomforts, and emotional guessing games, begin to feel hollow. You lose the appetite for passive aggression, for coded resentment disguised as politeness, for the exhausting dance of trying to decode what people won't say out loud. And perhaps most critically, you stop chasing validation from those who haven't yet clarified their signal. You recognize that approval from someone who can't see isn't affirmation. It's noise.

In that clearing, something rare begins to emerge. You start to build new relational structures, not necessarily with more people, but with the right ones. Friendships and partnerships become shaped not by shared illusions, but by shared discernment. You are drawn to people who are also doing the work of clarity, who aren't afraid to name what they see, who value directness over drama and curiosity over control. These relationships don't always look harmonious on the outside. They don't necessarily follow traditional templates. But there's a thread of mutual reality running through them. A thread that holds, even when things get uncomfortable.

And in that space of shared clarity, something deeper takes root, something that feels less like social cohesion and more like spiritual recognition. You begin to understand that absolute clarity, when extended between people, is a form of love. Not the sentimental kind that avoids tension in the name of peace, but the fierce kind that speaks truth in the service of freedom. It's the kind of love that doesn't turn away from someone's complexity. It meets them in it. It doesn't try to smooth over their rough edges; it honors the shape of who they are. It's the kind of presence that says, *I see you fully, not selectively. I know the signal behind the static. And I'm still here.*

This isn't about crafting perfect relationships, where everyone is always aligned or free of conflict. That would be another illusion. What it's about is creating relational spaces where signals can move unimpeded. Where perception is welcomed rather than deflected. Where truth is not wielded as a weapon, but offered as a gift, these are not easy dynamics to build, but once they form, they rewire your understanding of connection itself. You stop seeing truth as a risk to the relationship. You start seeing it as the relationship's foundation.

In a world that thrives on misunderstanding, that monetizes outrage, that teaches people to relate through image and implication rather than reality, these kinds of relationships are rare. They don't often trend. They don't produce viral moments. But they hold. They deepen. They endure. And that endurance is quietly revolutionary. Because when two people, or a group, commit to living with social clarity, they become islands of coherence in a sea of noise.

That's what clarity looks like when it moves beyond the mind and into the space between people. It's not just about individual thinking. It's about collective presence. A shared reality where distortion doesn't get the final word. Where love isn't confused with approval. Where staying means something. This is clarity, not as a private virtue, but as a relational force. Clarity, lived together.

Chapter 31: Clarity in Complexity

There is a kind of clarity that thrives in simplicity. It flows easily when choices are binary, outcomes are measurable, and truths are self-evident. But the real test of clean thinking isn't when everything lines up, it's when *nothing* does. When data conflicts, values compete, and no path is free from cost. This is the realm of **complexity**, and it's where most clarity collapses.

The temptation in complexity is to oversimplify. To turn mess into metrics. To flatten nuance into slogans. To cling to a narrative, not because it's true, but because it's *comforting*. And who can blame us? The human brain was not built for complexity. It was built for speed, for survival, for stories that resolve.

But clarity is not the same as simplicity. Absolute clarity does not mean removing all complexity. It means *perceiving it cleanly*, without distortion, projection, or panic.

Clarity in complexity begins with a fundamental shift: accepting that **ambiguity is not a failure of understanding**. It is often a feature of the system itself. In complex environments, markets, ecosystems, human emotions, and historical legacies, there are no clean edges. You cannot always disaggregate variables. You cannot always trace causality. And when you try to force that kind of reduction, you start to lie. Not maliciously. But you begin to shape reality to fit your frame, instead of letting your frame be reshaped by reality.

The disciplined thinker doesn't eliminate complexity. They learn to **navigate within it**.

This starts with **holding opposing truths**. The best thinkers don't need everything to agree. They can sit with the friction of contradictions. They can say, "This strategy is right for the company and wrong for the culture." Or, "This person is acting badly and still deserves compassion." Or, "This idea is both innovative and dangerous."

This isn't fence-sitting. It's **multidimensional thinking**. It's refusing the comfort of clarity that comes from cutting corners. You don't need to reduce complexity to get clear. You need to *see it without flinching*.

That requires a different kind of attention. In complexity, you don't look for answers. You look for **patterns**. For asymmetries. For second- and third-order effects. You watch how things interact, not just how they appear in isolation. You ask, "What's amplifying this? What's muting that? What would break if this changed?" You model scenarios, not solutions.

And you accept that in some cases, **there is no final truth, only better questions**.

That's hard for linear thinkers. It feels like failure. But in reality, it's a kind of maturity. The moment you stop demanding certainty is the moment you begin to perceive complexity with respect, not resistance.

Clarity in complexity also demands **slower cognition**. You can't brute-force insight. You need time for ideas to ferment, for your brain to map and remap without rushing to resolution. This is why so many bad decisions come from urgent contexts. Pressure speeds us up just when we should be slowing down.

Clean thinkers in complex systems learn to **protect cognitive spaciousness**. They sleep on decisions. They journal their confusion. They talk in loops, not ladders. They *return* to problems, rather than "solve" them. And in doing so, they gain a more profound clarity, not the clarity of resolution, but of orientation.

They start to sense where the center of gravity is. What's emerging. What's decaying? What tensions are permanent, and which are temporary? This is strategic clarity. You don't need to know the outcome. You need to *see what's shifting* and move accordingly.

This kind of clarity has another trait: it's **deeply aware of bias**. Complexity confuses people not just because it's hard, but because it triggers all the shortcuts we've built to survive information overload. We see what confirms us. We ignore what complicates our position. We jump to blame, because it's easier than mapping systems.

So, if you want clarity in complexity, you have to treat your perception as **suspect**. Not weak, just vulnerable to distortion. You cross-check your conclusions. You seek disconfirming evidence. You invite challenge not as critique, but as *refinement*. You don't trust clean stories that arrive too easily.

And most importantly, you avoid the seduction of the **clean villain**. In complexity, there's rarely one bad actor. Systems are shaped by incentives, by histories, by blind spots compounded over time. If your clarity depends on a scapegoat, it probably isn't clarity. It's just narrative discipline pretending to be truth.

What emerges from all this is a quieter kind of clarity. One that doesn't shout. One that doesn't promise easy wins. One that says: "This is what I can see clearly. This is what remains murky. And this is how I'll move, even without full visibility."

It's the clarity of an experienced navigator, not because the map is perfect, but because they've learned how to move when the fog never lifts entirely.

This kind of clarity feels different. It's not thrilling. It's grounding. It calms the noise without erasing the complexity. It lets you act, *without pretending the world is simple*.

And that, in the end, is what mature clarity looks like. Not less complexity, but *less confusion about how to move within it*.

Chapter 32: The Clarity Practice

You don't keep clarity. You *practice* it. That's the truth most people don't want to hear. They want the revelation to be enough. The retreat, the insight, and the perfect conversation are all meant to stick. To carry them forward without friction. But clarity is not a one-time state. It's a discipline. A loop. A lived rhythm.

It decays if you don't maintain it. Slowly, at first. A little more reactivity. A little more ambiguity in your speech. A little less patience in your thinking. You take shortcuts. You skip silence. You forget to question the frame. And just like that, the fog is back.

Which is why the thinkers who stay clear aren't the ones with the sharpest minds. They're the ones with the **strongest practices**.

They build environments that protect the signal. They reduce friction where it matters and increase friction where it counts. They don't just value clarity, they *train for it*.

What does that look like?

It starts with **daily clarity rituals**. Not rituals for performance, or productivity, but perception. You scan your mind in the morning: *What am I carrying that isn't mine? What am I assuming? What signal am I ignoring because it's inconvenient?* You create space for thought before you interface with the world. Sometimes that's a walk. Sometimes it's writing. Sometimes it's simply five minutes of stillness before the floodgates open.

Then, throughout the day, you protect your **cognitive environment**. That means editing your inputs. Not to live in a bubble, but to reduce ambient distortion. You don't scroll endlessly through outrage. You don't consume information at the rate others produce it. You *filter for signal*, ideas that challenge you cleanly, perspectives that sharpen you, voices that don't depend on fear to be heard.

And you track your state. You don't trust your thinking when you're exhausted, spun, or defensive. You don't force clarity when your mind is fogged by stress. You pause. You reset. You wait for cleaner ground. You don't treat yourself like a content machine. You treat yourself like an instrument, tuned, cared for, calibrated.

Over time, you develop an internal diagnostic. You *feel* when clarity is slipping. You sense it in your language, your posture, your reactivity. And because you've practiced returning, you don't panic. You don't catastrophize the slide. You get back to basics.

And at the end of the day, you **debrief the fog**. You reflect not just on what went wrong, but also on how you perceived it. Where were you cleaned? Where did you override your instinct? Where did you flinch from a truth? Where did you speak too soon, or too late?

You don't use this to shame yourself. You use it to *refine your awareness*. You become a student of your attention. You notice what triggers your distortions. What drains your discernment? What patterns bring out your sharpest mind?

And then, this is key: you build **relational clarity hygiene**. You don't just practice alone. You curate relationships that support clean perception. You surround yourself with people who reflect reality, not just approval. People who won't let you slide into performance. People who will question your assumptions *without turning it into a game of status*.

That kind of clarity loop is rare in friendships. Even rarer in teams. But when it's there, when everyone's committed to a shared signal, it creates a culture of coherence. Meetings don't spiral. Feedback doesn't trigger. Conflict becomes creative. And most importantly, people feel seen, not just for how they perform, but for how they *perceive*.

You can't fake that. You can't systematize it with tools alone. It has to be practiced. Daily. Consciously. Not with rigid rules, but with *repeating rhythms*. Not with ideology, but with intent.

And yes, there will be breaks. You'll lose your edge. You'll regress to noise. You'll say things you don't mean. You'll believe things that aren't true. That's inevitable. But if you've practiced the return, *if clarity is a muscle, not a mood*, you come back faster. You suffer less damage. You carry less shame.

That's the real power of clarity as a practice. It's not perfection. It's a *repair*.

You develop trust in your ability to recover. To re-see. To un-distort. To pause, recalibrate, and speak again, this time without the fog.

And that's what makes clarity sustainable. Not that you never lose it. But that you've built a life, a cadence, a culture, a set of agreements, that makes return possible. Not someday. But *today*.

You don't have to retreat to the mountains. You don't need silence chambers or infinite time. You need attention. You need commitment. You need the courage to name what's true *before* it calcifies into distortion.

You can live in a noisy world with a clean mind. But only if you're willing to practice. Every day. Every moment. Every breath.

Chapter 33: Clarity as Leadership

The most overlooked trait of authentic leadership isn't charisma, drive, or even vision. It's clarity. Not clarity of messaging or strategy, but clarity of *mind*. The kind that stabilizes a room before a single word is spoken. The kind that sees through the swirl of emotional currents, distorted incentives, and premature conclusions, not with arrogance, but with calm.

Because in a fogged world, leadership is not the loudest voice. It's the cleanest perception.

People often talk about leaders needing to "see around corners." But what does that mean? It means seeing through noise. It means discerning a signal when others are overwhelmed. It means knowing what *not* to react to, what can be safely ignored, so your energy stays directed toward the truly consequential.

Clarity, in this sense, becomes a form of **emotional gravity**. It grounds people. They feel safer in your presence, not because you promise perfect outcomes, but because you are not pulled into reactivity. The swirl of urgency, fear, or consensus does not control you.

But this kind of clarity isn't something you inherit with a title. It's something you cultivate, relentlessly, through the way you think when no one is watching. Through the decisions you revisit privately. Through the questions you ask yourself about motive, bias, and pressure. Through the discomfort, you're willing to face it when everyone around you is looking the other way.

Leadership clarity is forged in solitude and proven in public.

It starts with your relationship to reality. If you cannot see things clearly, you cannot lead others through them. If you are seduced by performance, you will mistake performance for progress. If you are afraid of disappointing people, you will design your decisions around avoidance instead of alignment. And if you are addicted to speed, you will destroy the very insight that makes your leadership valuable in the first place.

Clarity requires you to slow down long enough to separate urgency from importance. To distinguish the truth from the performance of truth. To tolerate not knowing long enough to hear what others missed. These are not soft skills. They are strategic capabilities.

And they are rare.

Because clarity is hard. Not technically hard. *Emotionally* hard. It forces you to confront the gap between your intent and your impact. It asks you to hold multiple truths at once: the data and the story, the feeling and the fact, the vision and the constraint. It demands that you think in layers, not lines.

Most people want simple answers. Leaders with clarity don't pander to their desires. They simplify the message, but not the thinking. They speak plainly, but they don't reduce complexity to empty slogans. They name the trade-offs. They acknowledge what's at stake. And they never pretend they're immune to distortion.

That's what makes them trustworthy.

Clarity in leadership is often mistaken for infallibility, for being the person in the room who always has the answer, who never hesitates, never backtracks, never reveals uncertainty. But that's not clarity, that's performance. Absolute clarity has nothing to do with perfection. It has everything to do with transparency. It's about knowing, and showing, how decisions are made. What principles are guiding them? What trade-offs are being accepted? Which feedback will shape future direction, and where might the current frame already be too narrow or outdated? Clarity in leadership means your process is intelligible, not always agreeable, not always flawless, but visible, coherent, and honest enough to be revised.

That kind of clarity doesn't remove conflict. It removes guesswork. People no longer have to read between the lines, hoping to decode unspoken rules or shifting priorities. They don't have to protect themselves with silence or posturing. They can trust the frame, not because it's unshakable, but because it's known. In a culture like that, psychological safety doesn't come from universal agreement; it comes from orientation. Everyone may not see the destination the same way, but they can at least know the compass you're using. And that clarity, that willingness to show your thinking even as it evolves, creates space for something rare: challenge without fear.

When a leader is clear, on purpose, on process, and on where their perspective might still be developing, others begin to meet that clarity with their own. They're not tiptoeing around egos or second-guessing motives. They can speak up, push back, and bring sharper data and stronger questions. Not to destabilize the leader, but to contribute meaningfully. What results isn't just higher morale. It's higher fidelity thinking. When people stop wasting energy on self-protection, they redirect that energy into sharper execution. And when clarity becomes cultural, not just concentrated at the top, the organization begins to move differently. Decisions get cleaner. Communication tightens. Blind spots shrink.

But this kind of clarity can't be mandated. It has to be modeled. And not just in high-stakes boardrooms or annual strategy sessions, but in small, everyday interactions, the kind that quietly shape the tone of everything else. How a leader handles contradiction when it surfaces in a meeting. How they sit with ambiguity when the path forward isn't obvious. How they respond when caught off guard, or when a junior team member raises a legitimate concern. How they speak when they don't yet have a resolution but still need to provide direction. These are the moments that build, or break, the culture of clarity.

You can't fake this. You can't script it in advance. It requires a kind of internal steadiness, a willingness to let others see you think, not just hear your conclusions. And that's a vulnerable stance. But it's also the most stabilizing one you can offer. Because when people see that you're willing to hold clarity without pretending to be infallible, they learn to do the same. You teach them, not through declarations, but through demonstration, that clear thinking is not brittle, it's dynamic. And that dynamic clarity is what allows entire systems to adapt, without losing integrity, even under pressure.

Leadership, then, becomes less about control and more about coherence. Not about having all the answers, but about building a context in which better answers can emerge. A context where people know what matters, learn how to contribute, and know how to challenge you without needing to tiptoe. That's the kind of leadership that doesn't just move fast, it moves forward. And that's the kind of clarity that scales.

Do they default to empty optimism, or do they name the unknown and keep going? Do they create more fog when they're stressed, or do they hold the line on clarity even under pressure?

These small moments accumulate. People are watching more closely than most leaders realize. And what they're watching for isn't just competence. It's *coherence*. Is what you say aligned with what you do? Is how you decide aligned with what you value?

This is why clarity is so threatening to people who benefit from confusion, because when a leader shows up with clean thought and coherent action, it reveals every distortion around them. It makes the invisible visible. It names what others have learned to ignore. It says: *This is what aligned decision-making looks like.* Not perfect. Not infallible. But *owned*.

And ownership is rare in fogged systems.

Leaders who operate this way don't need to signal confidence. It's felt. They don't need to dominate conversations. They ask better questions. They don't need to create urgency. They create *focus*. And when things go wrong, as they inevitably do, they recover clarity faster than most. They don't spiral into drama. They recalibrate, they recommit, and they move forward.

This is the real edge of clarity as leadership. It makes you less reactive. More precise. Less noisy. More potent. Your words carry more weight because they aren't trying to cover anything. Your presence does more work because you aren't scattered or performative. And your impact ripples farther because people don't just hear your message, they trust your perception.

Chapter 34: The Cost of Clarity

It's comforting to believe that clarity always pays off. The cleaner you think, the better your outcomes. That's when you strip away the distortion; people will thank you. That is when you see things as they are and act accordingly, the world will adjust itself around your wisdom.

But clarity has a cost.

It always has.

And pretending otherwise is how people get blindsided when the friction comes. Because the moment you begin to see clearly, truly clearly, not just selectively, the world does not applaud. At least, not right away. What often happens is something closer to social dissonance. Your clarity begins to reveal things that others have learned to ignore. And that revelation, no matter how gentle, can make people uncomfortable.

Clarity is not just a shift in how you perceive. It's a disruption in the consensus reality you once agreed to. It exposes unspoken contracts. It challenges implicit norms. It breaks the illusion of shared understanding that many relationships and institutions depend on to keep moving forward. So when you start naming what no one else will, or walking away from dynamics that no longer feel right, you are not just changing yourself. You are changing the system around you. And systems resist change.

That resistance is one cost.

You may be labeled difficult. Or uncooperative. Or intense. You may be told you're "overthinking" when you're just no longer willing to pretend. You may lose access to certain circles. Some people will retreat. Others will test you, pushing to see if your clarity holds or if it was just a phase. What they're testing is whether your new perception threatens their old comfort.

And even when they don't say it aloud, the message is clear: "Can't you just go back to how it was?"

But you can't.

Because once you've seen clearly, there's no clean way to unsee. You might be able to rejoin the performance for a while, but it will cost you. The price of pretending is paid in confusion, stress, and self-doubt. You'll start to fragment again. You'll stop trusting your signal. You'll feel off, not in a dramatic way, but in the quiet erosion of internal integrity.

The second cost is subtler: **loneliness**. Not permanent, not total. But real.

Clarity creates separation, at least for a while. It places you in that strange space between understanding the group and no longer being of it. You still care. You still feel connected. But you can no longer participate in the same way. You can't play the same games, laugh at the same stories, believe the same myths. You see too much. And that seeing isolates.

This doesn't mean you become superior. That's another trap. But it does mean you become *someone else*. And that shift can feel existential because clarity isn't just about being right. It's about standing alone in a moment when being wrong would be more socially convenient.

Many people collapse here. Not because they're weak, but because the pull of belonging is strong. And when clarity feels like exile, the temptation to surrender it becomes almost noble. "Maybe I'm being too harsh. Maybe I'm the problem. Maybe I should soften the edge a little."

But clarity doesn't mean cruelty. It just means precision. And if your clarity isolates you, it's not because you're better than others. It's because you're in a transitional space where the new alignment hasn't yet replaced the old one.

You're between worlds. The world of distortion that no longer fits, and the world of coherence that hasn't fully formed.

Hold steady.

The third cost is **emotional exposure**. When you see things clearly, you also see your past blindness. The patterns you tolerated. The compromises you justified. The roles you played. And it stings. It hurts to realize how long you've lived with noise, how many decisions you made from a fogged state. There's grief in clarity. Not just for what was lost, but for what you didn't even know you were missing.

And yet, this grief is sacred. It's how you metabolize your former self. It's how you release the part of you that needed distortion to survive. And that's not something to be ashamed of. That's growth. But it still costs something. You have to feel it. You have to let it move through you.

Only then does clarity become durable.

There's also the cost of **responsibility**. When you see clearly, you are now accountable for that seeing. You can no longer claim ignorance. You can no longer say, "I didn't know." You can't delegate decisions to others and pretend you were following orders. Clarity forces you to act. Or to knowingly choose inaction. But either way, the illusion of powerlessness dissolves.

And for many, that is terrifying.

Because with clarity comes consequence. Not just for others, but for yourself. You might have to walk away from what's comfortable. You might have to start over. You might have to admit you were wrong. And you might have to tell the truth when no one else will.

This is not a performance. This is personal.

Clarity will test your tolerance for ambiguity. It will test your loyalty to convenience. It will ask you to distinguish between what is true, what is easy, and what is aligned with expectations. It will force you to reckon with your inertia. And it will keep whispering, even when you wish it would stop.

There's a paradox that reveals itself only after you've lived through it enough times to stop resisting it. At first, the cost of clarity feels steep, unfair, and even. It stings to stand in truth when illusion is easier, more palatable, more socially acceptable. But with time, something shifts. The pain doesn't vanish, but it transforms. The sharp edge dulls into something bearable. And eventually, the price becomes not just tolerable, but integral. You begin to see it not as a penalty, but as proof. The friction no longer reads as failure or misalignment; it becomes the marker of something genuine. Something alive. Something that matters.

This is how it changes you. Not all at once, but gradually, insistently. You stop craving ease for its own sake. You start to notice how hollow comfort can feel when it's built on denial. The silence that used to soothe you now sounds suspicious. The smooth surface that once passed for success now triggers suspicion. You begin to prefer the tension that comes with truth, the discomfort that follows honesty, the unease that accompanies integrity. Because at least in those places, something real is happening. And once you've known that, illusion becomes not just unconvincing, it becomes intolerable.

You begin to find people who are wired the same way. Not because you're looking for them, but because the static you used to emit, the performative harmony, the evasive politeness, is gone. And in its place is coherence. Not perfection. Not omniscience. But a kind of wholeness that others can feel. The conversations change. The rooms you enter shift—the tolerance for superficiality drops. You start building structures, workflows, and relationships that don't rely on smoke and mirrors. You stop designing for appearances and begin shaping things that hold up under pressure—systems that reflect reality rather than distorting it for convenience or applause.

What becomes unmistakably clear, over and over again, is that the price of clarity is high. It will cost you comfort. It may cost you approval. It will often cost you the ability to blend in. But distortion comes with a steeper bill. It eats away at your confidence in subtle, corrosive ways. It turns straightforward choices into ambiguous landmines. It drains your vitality in the form of quiet dread, self-doubt, and emotional fatigue. And most insidiously, it creates a life that might pass all the external tests, status, income, and social ease, while internally feeling unmoored, misaligned, and false. Over time, that gap becomes a weight you can't carry. It demands to be closed.

So, you start paying the price, not out of some moral superiority or philosophical idealism. You pay it because there comes a point when you can't not. You've tasted the difference. You've felt what it's like to act from a place of grounded clarity, to move without the tremble of second-guessing, to speak without the residue of performative compromise. And once you've known that kind of inner alignment, quiet, firm, not needing to be validated, you can't go back to a life dictated by noise. You don't just want the truth. You require it.

Chapter 35: The Clean Mindset

Clarity isn't just a cognitive state. It's not something you "achieve" during a well-rested morning or in the wake of a profound insight. Those moments matter, but they aren't enough. Because clarity is fragile when it's treated as a temporary condition, it bends too easily under pressure. It dissolves when the context shifts. It fades the moment life gets messy again.

The deeper version of clarity, the one that lasts, is not a mood. It's a mindset. A way of orienting yourself toward the world. A commitment to thinking even when the environment is chaotic. It's a posture, not a destination. And like any real posture, it must be cultivated.

The clean mindset doesn't mean perfection. It begins with the radical acceptance that you will be wrong, that you will be biased, that you will be influenced in ways you don't immediately perceive. But rather than trying to eliminate these distortions through sheer force of discipline, the clean mindset builds a life that can *catch* them. It is designed for interruption. It creates friction in the right places. It puts up bumpers that keep you within a specific ethical and perceptual lane, even when your emotions threaten to override your cognition.

This mindset starts with **clarity as a value**, not just a tool. In most environments, clarity is treated as instrumental, something to access when making big decisions or when giving a presentation. But to truly live clean, clarity has to be elevated. It has to become something you protect in the small choices, not just the large ones.

It's in how you word an email, how you respond to passive aggression, and how you spend the first ten minutes of your day. These are not neutral acts. They either reinforce your mental cleanliness or erode it. The clean mindset understands that attention is sacred, that input shapes output, and that the quality of your decisions is a direct function of the quality of your awareness.

The clean mindset also means living in active resistance to mental clutter. Not asceticism. Not detachment. But active discernment. You choose what enters your head. You decide who influences your internal compass. You audit what you're absorbing and ask: *Is this signal or performance? Is this true or just loud?*

This doesn't make you cynical. It makes you surgical.

You don't waste energy debating things that don't matter. You don't play games where the rules are designed to confuse. You don't outsource your frame of reference to the collective emotion of the week. You anchor yourself. You opt out of the mental churn that passes for engagement. You care deeply, but selectively.

A clean mindset also recognizes the danger of unexamined repetition. Most mental mess isn't born from chaos; it's born from autopilot. You begin to respond to situations the way you always have. You inherit strategies, beliefs, and stories that once served a purpose but are now just residue. You think the way you were trained to believe. And you mistake that inheritance for truth.

Living clean means interrupting that default. It means checking your defaults before they become decisions. It means not confusing familiarity with alignment. The clean thinker doesn't just ask "what should I do?" They ask, "Where did this framework come from?" "Who does this benefit?" "What is the trade-off I'm not naming?"

This is not overthinking. It is sober navigation.

It also demands a different relationship to discomfort. Because clarity is often inconvenient, it rarely affirms all your desires at once. It doesn't always make you feel good. But it makes you feel whole. It grants coherence at the cost of comfort. And that cost is where many people retreat.

But the clean mindset doesn't see discomfort as a red flag. It sees it as a signal. A marker that you've left the safety of inherited thought and entered the terrain of actual insight. If you are not uncomfortable sometimes, you are not yet thinking for yourself.

Maintaining this mindset requires more than just good intentions. It requires *structure*. Not rigid systems, but supportive scaffolding. Rituals that return you to the center. Practices that sharpen your filter. People who challenge your bias instead of reinforcing it. Reflection spaces that let you clean your mental windshield without shame.

A clean thinker doesn't wait for overwhelm to recalibrate. They bake recalibration into their week. Into their decisions. Into their relationships. They normalize signal checks. They revisit choices not to ruminate, but to refine.

This becomes a way of life.

It also affects how you engage with others. A clean thinker doesn't manipulate through confusion. They don't tolerate passive fog in teams, in families, in organizations. They ask the tricky question. They invite disagreement. They bring clarity not just to their own choices, but to the collective ones.

And they don't do it to perform. They do it because confusion is costly. Because distortion is contagious. Because someone has to hold the clean edge when things get messy.

That someone is you.

Living this way does not mean you always know what to do. It means you know how to get back to yourself. It means you have a method, not just a mood. A muscle, not just a flash of brilliance. It means you can recover from distortion faster than you can withstand the fog without becoming fogged yourself.

The clean mindset is resilient. Not because it avoids mess, but because it doesn't *become* the mess. It lets you stay rooted while the world swirls. It enables you to perceive clearly without rushing to control. It allows you to lead, to build, to choose, not from panic, not from pressure, but from something more profound. Something durable.

In a world of distortion, this mindset becomes rare.

But it is available. It is buildable. And it is revolutionary in its quiet.

You won't always be thanked for holding it. But you will sleep better. You will think sharply. You will make decisions that you can stand by, even when the crowd changes its mind. And slowly, almost invisibly, you will start to change the world around you, not by force, not by noise, but by example.

Clarity, held this way, becomes not just a strategy, but a stance. A way of being. A way of seeing. A way of moving through the world that is clean, not because it is sanitized, but because it is *honest*.

That is the clean mindset.

And that is what lasts.

Reflection: Returning to the Body

- ∞ What does clarity feel like in your body? How does fog feel different?
- ∞ When do you override your body's signals, and why?
- ∞ What helps you return to groundedness, without escaping into thought?

Your clearest thinking may not come from your mind. It may begin in your spine, your breath, your pace.

Epilogue: The Clean Mind in a Dirty World

The world doesn't clean itself up for your clarity.

It won't slow down to accommodate your new way of thinking. It won't quiet itself to make space for your attention. It won't pause its onslaught of noise, pressure, crisis, and spectacle just because you've decided to live more deliberately. The world will remain as it is, messy, fast, contradictory, and full of distractions designed to derail your perception.

That's not pessimism. That's realism. And it matters, because many people who begin the pursuit of clarity believe, naively, that the outer world will respond to their inner changes. That once they learn to see more clearly, everything will become simpler, cleaner, and easier to manage. But it doesn't. The opposite is often true.

When you clean your lens, you don't erase complexity; you become more aware of it. You notice the contradictions you used to ignore. You see the tension others pretend isn't there. You feel the friction in conversations that once passed without a second thought. Clarity doesn't make the world lighter. It makes it *visible*, and that can be weighty.

This is why clarity isn't about comfort. It's about **capacity**.

It's not a technique to feel better, though it often reduces the anxiety that comes from confusion. It's not a weapon to out-argue others, though it can sharpen your words. It's not a brand of superiority, though some will accuse you of that. It's a *way of living in contact with reality*, even when reality is unresolved, even when it's painful, even when it costs you.

And it *will* cost you.

You'll lose some people. People who relied on your confusion to maintain their comfort. People who preferred your silence. People who mistook your clarity for judgment. You'll walk away from work that once looked promising because you can now see the trade-offs hiding behind the offer. You'll say no to meetings, platforms, habits, and relationships that once formed the scaffolding of your identity.

You'll say no more often, and with more peace.

But you'll also say yes, with more discernment, more alignment, more power.

That's what a clean mind offers you. Not a retreat from the world, but a new way of moving through it. You stop looking for clarity in the world's design. You start bringing it with you.

You become the one who can pause when others rush. Who can ask better questions when others default to certainty? Who can sit with the whole truth, not just the convenient part? Who can speak directly, even when it unsettles the room, not to provoke, but to illuminate. You model what it means to remain clear *without becoming cold*, sharp *without being harsh*, precise *without being cruel*.

That is rare. And it is needed.

Because we are drowning in fog. Fog of information. Fog of outrage. Fog of performance. Fog of passive aggression disguised as diplomacy. Fog of collective noise passed off as cultural wisdom.

And through that fog, people are trying to live. To love. To lead. To build things that matter. They are failing not because they are stupid, or weak, or unmotivated, but because they can't see enough to orient themselves.

They don't need better tools. They need a better **signal**.

And when someone steps into that space with a clear frame, when they speak from calm ground, when they cut through the noise with a clean question, when they name what's happening without moralizing or retreating, it's felt. Not as performance. Not as dominance. But as *truth carried lightly*.

That's what this book has been about. Not clarity as aesthetic, but clarity as commitment. Not purity, but perception. Not control, but coherence.

You do not graduate into permanent clarity. There is no pinnacle, no final peak from which you look out and see everything perfectly, forever. What you get, if you're honest and diligent, is a shifting edge, the boundary of your distortion. And while that edge never disappears entirely, it moves. With time, it drifts closer to the source of what's real. The static begins to thin. The fog doesn't vanish, but you start to recognize its patterns, its tells, its fingerprints. Your signal, the most genuine part of you, strengthens. You begin to feel it humming more clearly through the chaos. The lens you think through stays cleaner, longer. And even when it clouds, your recovery accelerates. Confusion doesn't derail you the way it used to. Crisis doesn't send you into hiding. Failure doesn't brand you as broken. Instead, you learn the way back. You practice the return. And slowly, it becomes your second nature.

To live with a clean mind in a dirty world is not to be untouched by the filth. It's about recognizing it, naming it, and staying intact anyway. It's to see without collapsing under the weight of what you see. It's to think while others panic. To choose even when the ground is shifting. It's not the absence of pain or fear or contradiction; it's the ability to sense what's real through all of that and act from it anyway. Not because you're fearless, but because you trust the part of you that sees. And that trust? It isn't granted by a degree, or endorsed by a system, or coded into an app. No certificate confirms you've earned it. It's forged internally. Quietly. Relentlessly. In the choices you make when no one's watching. In the small moments when your alignment gets tested, by conflict, by silence, by pressure. You calibrate there. You return there.

And if you keep returning, if you stay in a relationship with what's true, not what's convenient, not what's performative, not what earns you applause, you don't just think differently. You begin to live differently. You choose the kind of work that doesn't bend your values into something unrecognizable. You stop auditioning for love. You no longer need every interaction to reflect your worth. You create not to prove something, not to fill some hollow, but because you can't not. You learn to build systems, internal and external, that don't rely on illusion to function. You build structures that don't require you to fracture yourself to maintain them. You begin to exist in a way that others feel before they understand. And slowly, you leave behind a different kind of residue. Not confusion. Not noise. But clarity. A clarity that doesn't shout or posture. A clarity that spreads, not by force, but by presence. From one clean mind to another.

The fog doesn't leave. It never promised to. But you don't go either. You stay. You learn to see through it, not with some grand enlightenment, but with a practiced resilience. And that, in the end, is the quiet triumph. Not that you escaped the mess, but that you found a way to live cleanly inside it.

About the Author

Avery Keene is a former strategist turned clarity coach, known for helping high-performing thinkers cut through noise, reclaim mental sovereignty, and navigate complexity without collapse. Drawing on a background that spans behavioral psychology, systems design, and trauma-informed leadership, Keene's work blends hard-edged insight with lived wisdom.

For over a decade, Keene advised founders, operators, and policy leaders behind the scenes, helping them make cleaner, higher-leverage decisions under pressure. Now, through writing and private counsel, Avery offers frameworks for thinking clearly in a world addicted to speed, overstimulation, and illusion.

The Book On Clarity is not Keene's first book, but it's the one most needed for this moment.

When not writing or working with clients, Avery prefers long walks without headphones, ugly first drafts, and conversations that get somewhere real.

About The Publisher

Welcome to The Book On Publishing

At The Book On Publishing, we believe in rewriting the rules of learning. Whether you're chasing your next big idea, building a better life, or simply curious about what should have been taught in school, you've come to the right place.

We're a platform built for dreamers, doers, and lifelong learners, offering bold, practical books and tools that empower you to take charge of your journey. From real-world skills to mindset mastery, we publish the book on what matters.

No fluff. No lectures. Just what you need to know, delivered with clarity, purpose, and a spark of curiosity.

Start exploring. Start growing. Start writing your story.

Read more at https://thebookon.ca.

Acknowledgment of AI Assistance

Portions of this book were developed with the support of AI. While every word has been carefully reviewed and refined by the author, AI served as a valuable tool for brainstorming, editing, and structuring ideas. Its assistance helped accelerate the creative process and bring clarity to complex topics.